George Weidenfeld and Nicolson Limited/Arthur Barker Limited

Weidenfeld (Publishers) Limited

Registered office 91 Clapham High Street, London SW4 7TA   *Telephone* 01-622 9933
Registered number 395166 England   *Telegrams and cables* Nicobar London SW4 7TA   *Telex* 918066

Henry Root Esq.,
139 Elm Park Mansions
Park Walk
London SW10   13 June 1979

Dear Mr Root,

Many thanks for your letter of 8 June to Lord Weidenfeld. I'm
glad to say the noble lord is far too busy making multi-million
dollar deals to read anything from no-hopers, and gets oppressed
minions like me to fob them off as politely as possible.

I would like to congratulate you on your book and make you an offer
you'll find hard to refuse. In return for £200,000 or a tankful
of petrol (whichever is the greater) we'd be delighted to publish
it. I give you a personal guarantee that under no circumstances
would we print less than six copies or remainder it within two
weeks of publication. You can't be fairer than that, now, can you?

I very much look forward to receiving your cheque by return of post.
I should say that we're currently reviewing our accounting procedures
and for safekeeping you'd be wise to make it out to **me personally**.

Yours ever,

Simon Dally

Simon Dally

PS   Do give my love to Nigs when you're next down at the Daily Mail.
     Tell him he's a naughty boy to be in both our pockets! You can't
     serve two masters in my view.

PPS No, our address isn't all right. But I'm looking forward to
     examining vacant Bloomsbury properties just as soon as I receive
     your cheque.

The Henry Root Letters

I WISH to protest most strongly about everything. --Henry Root, Park Walk, West Brompton.

EVENING STANDARD, WEDNESDAY, AUGUST 15, 1979

To Mrs Root and Mrs Thatcher: two ordinary mothers.

The Henry Root Letters

Henry Root

Weidenfeld and Nicolson
London

ISBN 0 297 77762 9

Printed in Great Britain by Butler & Tanner Ltd,
Frome and London

139 Elm Park Mansions
Park Walk
London, S.W.10.

Sir David McNee,
New Scotland Yard
London, S.W.1.   21st March 1979.

Dear Sir David,

Hang on! Ignore the media! Ordinary folk are with you all
the way in your campaign for greater police powers.

Better that ten innocent men be convicted than that one
guilty man goes free! That's what the lounge-room revolutionaries
fail to understand.

Don't be depressed by the fact that your 'image' isn't too
clever just yet. We have to face it that you come across a wee
bit charmless. So what? Do we want this once great country to
be policed by the likes of Mr Victor Sassoon the barber and cos-
metics expert from Los Angeles?

Your predecessor, Sir Robert Mark, was an accomplished PR
man, so it was easy for him. And he had a lot of luck with the
'Spaghetti House Siege Situation'. The public really liked that.
What a pity the recent 'Gunman Holed Up In Village Pub Shot Dead
By 392 Policemen Situation' didn't happen on your patch! That
would have been just the break you needed. As it was, the Chief
Constable of Essex was able to pick up the apples on that one.
Never mind. Your chance will come.

Here's a pound. Use it to enforce Law and Order.

So - you're doing your poor best, but what can we, the
ordinary folk, do? We need you to tell us. The politicians
(with the exception of Mrs Thatcher) aren't giving us a lead.

Could you oblige with a photo? I'd like to stick it up in
my boy Henry Jr's room in lieu of one of a popular crooning group
entitled The Boomtown Rats. The lad's 15, but he's not shaping
up. He idles around in his room all day, sewing sequins onto his
disco pumps and worse. When I put a photo of Sir Robert Mark on
his wall, it was down within seconds and up went the Boomtown
crooners again. I'm not usually an advocate of unauthorised
violence, but if he takes your picture down I'll knock the wee
blighter senseless, that's for sure.

Keep hammering 'em!

Support Mrs Thatcher!

Yours for greater police powers!

Henry Root

Henry Root.

COMMISSIONER OF POLICE
OF THE METROPOLIS

NEW SCOTLAND YARD
BROADWAY LONDON SW1H OBG

29 March 1979

Sir David McNee QPM

Dear Mr Root

The Commissioner has asked me to write and thank you for your letter of 21 March; your kind comments are appreciated.

As requested, I enclose a signed photograph of Sir David. Perhaps I should warn you, however, that the Commissioner keeps a close watch on crime reports and will be keeping a particular eye on them to ensure that you do not do what you propose to do should your son take the photograph off his wall!

I regret that police are not permitted to accept money for the purpose you propose; although the thought is acknowledged I have to return your donation herewith.

Yours sincerely

Brian Gittins
Private Secretary

Mr Henry Root
139 Elm Park Mansions
Park Walk
LONDON SW10

139 Elm Park Mansions
Park Walk
London, S.W.10.

Mrs Margaret Thatcher,   23rd March 1979.
The House of Commons,
London, S.W.1.

Dear Leader!

So they said a woman couldn't do it! They were forgetting
Joan d'Arc, the maid of Orleans! She put it over the French with
their bidets and so-called soixante-neuf and so will you!

Never give up!

This is what we've got to do. With the help of the Scot
Nats we can bring down Mr Callaghan and his ramshackle crew of
wooly-minded lightweights. At the first suitable opportunity
we must table a motion of no confidence in the Government. I'll
have to leave this to you. As long as you get your sums right
Jim'll be back feeding his pigs and you'll be measuring for new
curtains at No 10!

Throughout the coming battle I'll keep you in touch with
door-step opinion.

Avarice is patriotic! Here's a pound.

Your man on the door-step,

Henry Root

Henry Root.

PS.   Freedom to do as we're told under the law! Let's go!

139 Elm Park Mansions
Park Walk
London, S.W.10.

Mrs Margaret Thatcher,
The House of Commons,
London, S.W.1.   29th March 1979.

Dear Leader!

        Congratulations! You took my advice, you went for the vote
of no confidence and now you can start thinking about new colour
schemes for No 10!

        I believe 'Sunny Jim' is collecting his cards from Her
Majesty today. How nice for her to know it's the last she'll
be seeing of _him_ for a while! She must be looking forward to
cosy tea-time chats with another woman such as yourself. Two
mothers.

        Now, with great respect, a word of advice from an old
campaigner. It's been my experience that the weaker sex (God
bless 'em!) sometimes hesitate to go for the kill. I'm sure
this doesn't apply to you, but now is _not_ the time to back off.
You've shaken up 'Sunny Jim' with a stiff left hook and now
you've got to dump him on his backside with a solid right cross.
The old one-two. That's a boxing term. Get your husband, Mr
Thatcher, to explain it to you. I read an article about him in
'The Evening Standard' the other day. He sounds like a nice old
stick and I think we'd get on well together. The article said
he's a simple man who believes in calling a spade a spade. So
do I.

        Talking about spades, I gather you have one in your Shadow
Cabinet - the ex-Gurkha, Mr John Nott. Okay. Fair enough. Nothing
wrong with that. Trying to trick in some of the immigrant vote
by having one of our Asian friends in your inner circle is a
shrewd move on your part. But don't carry the concept too far.
Once you've won the election, ditch him.

        Another word of advice. In the coming campaign, _don't
worry_ about _your_ _voice_. Don't listen to people who say you
sound like a suburban estate agent's wife. What's wrong with
suburban estate agents? They have a vote!

        One last thing. Mrs Root and I have recently formed 'The
Ordinary Folk Against Porn Society'. We meet once a week with
some of our friends (Dr Littlewinkle and his good lady, the
Smithsons, Major Dewdrop and Fred and Rita Snipe, who live opposite, form the hard-core nucleus) to discuss sex, drugs, nudity
and violence. While I know these are all subjects that interest
you, I expect you'll be too busy at the moment, what with one
thing and another, to address us yourself. Don't worry. We
understand. However, a signed photograph and message of encour-
agement would mean a lot to our members.

        Don't forget the old one-two!

        Your Man on the Door-step!

        Henry Root
        Henry Root.

The Rt. Hon. Mrs. Margaret Thatcher, M.P.

HOUSE OF COMMONS
LONDON SWIA 0AA

4th April 1979

Dear Mr Root,

Mrs Thatcher has asked me to thank you for your
two recent letters of 23rd and 29th March.

She has asked me to say how grateful she is to
you for your kind donation and your very kind
words of support.   As you request I am sending
a photograph of Mrs Thatcher, which she has
signed for you.

As far as your request for a message is concerned,
I am afraid because of the forthcoming campaign
Mrs Thatcher has so many pressures on her time
that it is not possible for her to write one
personally.

She hopes you will understand the reasons
for this reluctant refusal, and asked me to
pass on her best wishes.

Yours sincerely,

Richard Ryder
Private Office

Henry Root Esq

139 Elm Park Mansions
Park Walk
London, S.W.10.

The Chairman,   23rd March 1979.
Faber & Faber Ltd,
London, W.C.1.

Dear Sir,
        Subject to certain stipulations, I'd be prepared to accept
the post of commissioning editor, as advertised in 'The Spectator'
this week.

        I had my people check you out thoroughly and I have to tell
you they ran into a lot of negative feedback. The word on the
literary scene is that the once respected name of Faber and Faber
isn't too sweet just now.

        Never mind. I can stop the rot. Books aren't my business,
but that's neither here nor there these days. Basic commercial
principles are the same whether you're selling poetry or wet fish
(my dodge, as it happens.) Don't get me wrong. I rub along all
right with books. In fact I quite like them. The trouble is
they don't like me. Still, who reads books? You've got to div-
ersify, up-date the product, smarten up the image - or go to the
wall.

        Who's selling really BIG now? Writers? Not a chance! The
punters are buying Ustinov, Niven, Betty Bacall, Diana Dors, Dr
J.P.R. Williams, Sir Robert Mark, Lady Antonia Fraser as was, Ted
Heath, Shirley Conran (the cook) and the vet from the Midlands.

        Have you the faintest idea how many copies of David Niven's
books have sold world-wide to date? 9½ million! That means there's
a hell of a lot of mugs out there, and we've got to reach them!

        I can show you how. Of course we'll run into a lot of
trouble with the grey-beards on your board and I'm afraid they'll
have to go. Leave this to me. As I say, my background is business systems and wet fish and I'm happy to be the goon with the
big hatchet.

        I've a lot of solid contacts abroad - particularly in Ice-
land, South Africa, Rhodesia, Turkey and Chile - and a stack of
valid ideas which could put you back on the literary map.

        As luck would have it I'll be in your neck of the woods
on Tuesday 3rd April, so unless I hear that it would be inconvenient for you I'll hop through your door at about 12.30.

        We can tie up the details (salary, expenses etc) then.

        Yours faithfully,

        Henry Root

        Henry Root.

Charles Monteith, Chairman. Matthew Evans, Managing Director.

T. E. Faber. A. T. G. Pocock.

Rosemary Goad. Giles de la Mare. G. W. Taylor.

Secretary: J. D. F. Nichols

FABER AND FABER LTD

PUBLISHERS

3 Queen Square, London WC1N 3AU   Fabbaf London WC1   01-278 6881

Telex: 299633 (FABER G)

HMS   28th March, 1979

Henry Root, Esq.,
139 Elm Park Mansions,
Park Walk,
London, S.W.10.

Dear Mr. Root,

We are grateful to you for having answered our advertisement
about the editorial vacancy here. We had a very large number of replies
and we have now compiled a short list of those people whom we would
like to interview. I very much regret to have to let you know that,
after having considered your application very carefully, we have
decided not to include your name on this list.

Do please let me say again how grateful we are to you for having
written to us.

Yours sincerely,

Henrietta Smyth

Henrietta Smyth
Secretary to the Chairman

P.S. The Chairman has asked me to add that there would be no point in
your calling in here on Tuesday morning, though he is grateful to you
for your offer to do so.

Registered Office as above. Registered in England. No. 944703

139 Elm Park Mansions
Park Walk
London, S.W.10.

Mr James Anderton,
The Chief Constable,
Greater Manchester,
Manchester.

23rd March 1979.

Dear Chief Constable,

Your stand against the porno merchants of Manchester is
an inspiration to ordinary folk down here in the soft south. Our
own Sir David McNee is doing his poor best, but the odds are
against him. He's a fine man, but the Hampstead pansies have
got him by the tail.

We have to keep asserting that people commit crimes not
because they come from so-called deprived backgrounds, but because
they're <u>wicked</u>. The statistics showing that only .000137% of
all crimes of senseless violence are carried out by stockbrokers
living in Sunningdale prove only that such folk are stockbrokers
because they've got a sense of right and wrong - not vice versa.

Since it's always been my opinion that the fight against
evil shouldn't be left entirely to intellectuals like yourself,
but that the man in the street should play his part too, Mrs Root-
and I recently formed 'The Ordinary Folk Against The Rising Tide
Of Filth In Our Society Situation Society' (TOFATRTOFIOSSS for
short). We meet once a week for a lively, no-holds-barred discussion over wine and cheese and a guest intellectual delivers
a short paper.

We have extended invites to most of the top turns in the
struggle against filth, many of whom will be familiar to you from
joint porn-monitoring talk-ins. I'm referring, of course, to
Lord Longford, Mary Kenny, Mrs Whitehouse, Mr Philip Wrack, the
Dowager Lady Birdwood, Mr Richard West and Sir Emile Littler (or
Prince Littler, as he now is, having inherited the title from
his brother.) So far we've drawn a complete blank, alas. It's
the old story. Intellectuals are very handy with words; less
handy, in my experience, when it comes to a bit of direct action.

I realise that cracking down on the porno merchants in
Manchester must take up a lot of your time, but is there any
chance that you might read us a paper? We would, of course, pay
your travelling expenses from Manchester and back.

Keep hitting 'em where it hurts!

'What Manchester thinks today, Hampstead will think in
ten years time!' (Richard West.)

Your pal in the soft south,

Henry Root

Henry Root.

C James Anderton Q.P.M., F.B.I.M.
Chief Constable

Chief Constable's Office
P O Box 22 (S.West PDO)
Chester House
Boyer Street
Manchester M16 0RE
Telephone 061-872 5050

27th March 1979.

Dear Mr. Root,

Thank you for your very kind letter
of support which I was most pleased to receive.

Much as I would like to support you
and your friends in your worthwhile cause, I
regret it will not be possible for me in the
foreseeable future to give any address in
London or, indeed, elsewhere. My diary of
speaking engagements is practically full until
the end of 1980.

Thank you for writing to me.

Yours sincerely,

Chief Constable.

H.Root, Esq.,
 139 Elm Park Mansions,
     Park Walk,
         London.S.W.10.

139 Elm Park Mansions
Park Walk
London, S.W.10.

Sir Robert Mark,
c/o William Collins & Sons Ltd,   26th March 1979.
14 St James's Place,
London, S.W.1.

Dear Sir Robert,
        It was with a deep sense of shock and outrage that I read
in 'The Daily Telegraph' recently that you are now driving a
breakdown van for the AA and selling life assurance in the evening.
        Surely your book, 'In the Office of Constable', didn't sell
that badly? I thought it was good! It could have done with a
few more anecdotes, perhaps, along the lines of the amusing incident early in your career when you had at a fellow in the water-
works and then broke his leg. That's the sort of stuff the public
likes. Shows the boys in blue to be human like the rest of us.
Perhaps it was an isolated incident. I dare say that sort of
excitement is just the glamorous side of a policeman's job.
        Anyway, here's a pound. Not much, I'm afraid, but if ord-
inary folk everywhere donated a pound to public servants on their
retirement they wouldn't be reduced in their declining years to
patrolling the M4 in a yellow van and selling life-assurance door-
to-door.
        Yours for a better deal for our distressed old folk!

        Henry Root

        Henry Root.

139 Elm Park Mansions
Park Walk
London, S.W.10.

The Rt Hon William Whitelaw,
The House of Commons,   28th March 1979.
London, S.W.1.

Dear Mr Whitelaw,
        As an ordinary father, I have been much disturbed by two
recent remarks by men in public life.
        First, in an interview in 'The Evening News', Sir Robert
Mark said that he would not be against the decriminalisation of
of cannabis as long as he could be convinced that the substance
had no harmful effects!
        Secondly, ex-Chief Superintendant so-called 'Nipper' Reed
said in the course of a TV interview with Mr Ludovic Kennedy
that when he was a serving officer it had been impossible to
investigate serious crimes from Scotland Yard due to the fact
that more criminals ran their affairs from there than did up-
holders of law and order! To catch the so-called Krays he had
been compelled to do all his phoning from a kiosk on the corner!
        With regard to Sir Robert's amazing observation, small
wonder this once great country continues to career down-hill
like a greased pig if ex-public servants can openly advocate
the decriminalisation of a pleasure for no better reason than
that it's harmless!
        And the alarming significance of Mr Reed's remark seems
to have gone unnoticed. Is it not on all fours with saying that
the last place at which one can safely mail a letter is the
Post Office?
        Can you give me your assurance, Sir, as our future Home
Secretary, that cannabis will not be legalised <u>however harmless
it turns out to be</u> and that under your firm stewardship the
police will once again have as much time to investigate crime .
as they now have to investigate each other?
        Support Mrs Thatcher!
        Yours Against the Decriminalisation of Harmless Pleasures!

        Henry Root

        Henry Root.

From: The Rt. Hon. William Whitelaw, C.H., M.C., M.P.

HOUSE OF COMMONS
LONDON SWIA OAA

2nd April, 1979

Dear Mr. Root,

Thank you for your letter of 28th March
and your very kind good wishes to our Party and
to Margaret Thatcher.

There is no question of any future Conservative
Government legalising cannabis. We also intend to
build up the strength and the quality of the Police
to give them a better oppo tunity to investigate
and prevent crime.

Yours sincerely,

[signature]

H. Root, Esq.,
139 Elm Park Mansions,
Park Walk,
London S.W.10.

139 Elm Park Mansions
Park Walk
London, S.W.10.

Ms Esther Rantzen,   26th March 1979.
BBC Television,
London, W.12.

Dear Esther,
        Congratulations on anther great show last night! The main 'How
to get your knickers off' item was hilarious! Both Mrs Root and I
chuckled all the way through it.

        You've got the formula just right. If only more people in TV
(television) realised that it's possible to be healthily vulgar without
descending to schoolboy smut.

        I enclose some humorous definitions and a comical poem for Cyril.
I hope you can use them. On the assumption that you can, I'm invoicing
the BBC separately.

        Humorous Definitions.
        Falsies: An enhancer to a maiden's pair!
        The Vatican: House of pill refute!
        The three ages of man: Tri-weekly, try weekly and try weakly!
        Graffiti in Gents' W.C.: Squatters' writes!

        Comical Poem.
        While Titian was mixing rose-madder,
        His model posed nude on a ladder.
        Her position to Titian
        Suggested coition,
        So he climbed up the ladder and had 'er!

        Just one slight criticism of the show last night. I thought your
dress was rather revealing for what is essentially family viewing. One
could see your legs quite clearly. I hope you won't mind my saying
this. One doesn't want to see women's legs in one's lounge-room at a
time when youngsters are still up and about.

        Could you possibly oblige with a photo?

        Yours for A Comical Definition!

        Henry Root

        Henry Root.

Henry Root.
139 Elm Park Mansions
Park Walk
London, S.W.10.

The Accounts Department
The BBC
Broadcasting House
Portland Place
London, W.1.

26th March 1979.

INVOICE

To four humorous definitions and one comical poem for
THAT'S LIFE...£12.95.

Kindly remit and oblige.

BRITISH BROADCASTING CORPORATION
BBC TV
KENSINGTON HOUSE RICHMOND WAY LONDON W14 0AX
TELEPHONE 01-743 1272   TELEX: 265781
TELEGRAMS AND CABLES: TELECASTS LONDON TELEX

REF: SLER

22/4/79

Dear Mr. Root,

Thank you very much indeed for taking the trouble to
write to me. Hearing from viewers like yourself is a
tremendous morale boost for us all - it really makes a
great difference to me to know that you find our work
enjoyable and worthwhile. May I send you my best wishes,
and thank you again for your letter.

Yours sincerely,

M' Esther Rantzen

The Accounts Department
The BBC
Broadcasting House
Portland Place
London, W.1.

139 Elm Park Mansions
Park Walk
London, S.W.10.

9th April 1979.

Dear Sir,

On 26th March I sent you an invoice for £12.95 for some humorous definitions and a comical poem I submitted to 'That's Life'.

I have not received the money and I must tell you that unless I get satisfaction by return of post I will be compelled to put the matter in the hands of my solicitor.

Yours faithfully,

Henry Root.

Henry Root.

BBC tv
BRITISH BROADCASTING CORPORATION
KENSINGTON HOUSE RICHMOND WAY LONDON W14 0AX
TELEPHONE 01-743 1272   TELEX: 265781
TELEGRAMS AND CABLES: TELECASTS LONDON TELEX

Mr H Root
139 Elm Park Mansions
Park Walk
London SW10

22nd April 1979

Dear Mr Root

Your letter of the 9th April 1979 has been forwarded to me by the BBC Accounts Department.

The That's Life programme does not pay fees for uncommissioned material that is not transmitted.

Yours sincerely

Henry Murray
Producer, That's Life

139 Elm Park Mansions
Park Walk
London, S.W.10.

Ms Esther Rantzen,
'That's Life',
Television Centre,
London, W.12.   23rd April 1979.

Dear Esther,
     You're a fat idiot and your show's a disgrace.
     Yours sincerely,

     Henry Root

     Henry Root.

BRITISH BROADCASTING CORPORATION
KENSINGTON HOUSE RICHMOND WAY LONDON W14 0AX
TELEPHONE 01-743 1272   TELEX: 265781
TELEGRAMS AND CABLES: TELECASTS LONDON TELEX
BBC TV

REF: SLER

Dear Mr. Root,

          26/4/79

     Thank you very much indeed for taking the trouble to
write to me. Hearing from viewers like yourself is a
tremendous morale boost for us all - it really makes a
great difference to me to know that you find our work
enjoyable and worthwhile. May I send you my best wishes,
and thank you again for your letter.

     Yours sincerely,

     Esther Rantzen

     pp Esther Rantzen

NO REPLY!

139 Elm Park Mansions
Park Walk
London, S.W.10.

Ray Cooney Esq,
The Whitehall Theatre,
London, S.W.1.   29th March 1979.

Dear Cooney,

　　Mrs Root and I saw your show 'Ipi Tombi' last night.　Better
late than never!　We both thoroughly enjoyed it and the nudity, being
ethnic, was for once entirely inoffensive.　I hope you won't mind
my saying this.　I assume from your name that you yourself are one
of our coloured friends.　Nothing wrong with that.　Good luck to you!

　　Anyway, it struck me that a hit show must make quite a handy
profit.　Do you look for outside investors - fairies, I think you
call them?

　　The fact is I've been in fish all my life, I've worked hard,
saved hard and now I reckon I could afford a small flutter without
breaking the bank.　I'm talking about just a **few thousand, spread**
over several shows to minimise the risk.　I believe the accident rate
is quite high in your business.

　　I hope you won't mind my asking.　I'd really appreciate the
opportunity to invest if it's at all possible, and I'd like to en-
courage someone from your part of the world.

　　I look forward to hearing from you.

　　Yours sincerely,

　　Henry Root

　　Henry Root.

139 Elm Park Mansions
Park Walk
London, S.W.10.

Michael Edwardes Esq,
British Leyland Ltd,
Marylebone Road,
London, N.W.1.   31st March 1979.

Dear Mr Edwardes,

As a patriot, I am becoming increasingly distressed by the fact
that the mere mention of 'British Leyland' by a music-hall comedian
gives rise to gales of ignorant laughter, rather as the conjoined
notions of Her Royal Highness Princess Anne and a horse are liable
to take the roof off the London Palladium if mentioned from the stage
in the course of one of Lord Delfont's Royal Variety Shows.

I would remind you, Sir, that every time someone laughs at
'British Leyland' they are laughing at Great Britain.

In the circumstances I would earnestly suggest that you change
the name of the company either to 'Japanese Leyland' or to 'Jamaican
Leyland'.

The only jokes ever made about the Japanese concentrate round the
fact that they tend to be extremely small (like yourself – nothing
wrong with that) and that they are clever little monkeys who work too
hard.

Jokes along these lines would only be good for your company's
image. And if jokes were made about 'Jamaican Leyland' you could
prosecute the offenders under the Race Discrimination Act.

I look forward to hearing your reaction to this suggestion.

Yours sincerely,

Henry Root

Henry Root. Patriot!

139 Elm Park Mansions
Park Walk
London, S.W.10.

D. Dudley Morgan Esq,
Theodore Goddard & Co,   7th April 1979.
16 St Martin-le-Grand,
London, E.C.1.

Dear Mr Morgan,

Your firm has been recommended to me as being one with some
experience of the law. I address myself to you personally as
the senior partner since I have litigation of some import to prosecute and I don't wish to find myself in the hands of the office-
boy.

As the enclosed documents will show, I wrote to Mr Michael
Edwardes of British Leyland on 31st March with the viable suggestion that the name of the company be changed to 'Japanese Leyland'.

As you will imagine, it was with a sense of outrage that I
discovered on 4th April that my concept was already in the pipe-
line. By 5th April the matter had become public knowledge, as
the enclosed cartoon will adequately demonstrate.

Mr Edwardes has not favoured me with the courtesy of a
reply to my letter and I am now persuaded that he is of a mind
to 'borrow' my notion without acknowledgement or payment.

You will agree that in the circumstances damages of unusual
consequence would come my way in the High Court.

I look forward to hearing that you will act for me in this
matter. I am in a position to put further work your way pursuant
to a satisfactory assessment of your performance hereunder.

Yours faithfully,

Henry Root

Henry Root.

THEODORE GODDARD & CO.

D. DUDLEY MORGAN
PETER A J. MORLEY
J. N. FISHER
R. DEREK FOX
BLANCHE H. M. A. LUCAS
MARÉ N. STACEY
MICHAEL Q. WALTERS
F. J. CALDERAN
R. K. SHUTE
M. J. W. TOD
EDWIN A. JONES
WILLIAM S. ROGERS
M. A. CROFT BAKER
M. J. HARRIS

ANTONY HEALD
CHRISTOPHER CLOGG
W. H. STUART MAY
ANDREW BINGHAM
MARTIN G. CHESTER
P. GRAFTON GREEN
DIANA GUY
DAVID S. WILKINSON
R. M. PRESTON
DEREK W LEWIS
SIMON STUBBINGS
MARTIN KRAMER
GUY I. F. LEIGH

R. DEREK WISE C.B.E. (RESIDENT IN PARIS)
EDWARD WILTSHIRE (RESIDENT IN MADRID)

CONSULTANT
DEREK F. S. CLOGG
ASSOCIATES

E. A. CLARKE
A. R. W. CARRINGTON
C. J. J. MAPLES

DIANA SNEEZUM
NICHOLAS WHITMEY

16 ST. MARTIN'S-LE-GRAND

LONDON EC1A 4EJ

Telephone: 01-606 8855
Cables: Assumpsit London E.C.1
Telex: 884678
Telegrams: Assumpsit London Telex
Telecopier Extension 208
L.D.E. and C.D.E. Box Number 47
Stock Exchange Number STX 2346

Associate Offices:

167 RUE DE L'UNIVERSITE
PARIS 75007
Telephone: (010 331) 705 89 45
Telex: 250661

LAGASCA 106
MADRID 6
Telephone: (010 34 1) 275 03 24
Telegrams: Interlex

17 BOND STREET
ST. HELIER, JERSEY C I
Telephone: (0534) 36676
Telex: 41689

Your Ref

Our Ref 21

H. Root, Esq.,
139 Elm Park Mansions,
Park Walk,
London, S.W.10.

12th April, 1979.

Dear Sir,

Thank you for your letter of 7th April with enclosures concerning your possible complaint against Mr. Michael Edwards of British Leyland. I do not think I would necessarily agree with the penultimate paragraph of your letter that in the circumstances considerable damages would be awarded to you in the High Court.

In the circumstances this would not be a case which this firm would be prepared to undertake, and had we been prepared to do so we would have required very substantial sums on account before we accepted any instructions. If you still wish to proceed I suggest you seek some other firm who will be prepared to accept your instructions.

Yours faithfully,

D. DUDLEY MORGAN

139 Elm Park Mansions
Park Walk
London, S.W.10.

Eric Levine Esq,
Eric Levine & Co,
63 Lincoln's Inn Fields,   17th April 1979.
London, W.C.2.

Dear Mr Levine,

I would like to instruct you in two pertinent matters.

As the enclosed letter will show, I wrote to Mr Michael
Edwardes of British Leyland on 31st March suggesting that the
name of the company be changed to 'Japanese Leyland'. It was
with a deep sense of outrage that I discovered through 'the
media' on 4th April that my concept had been taken up and acted
on. By 5th April the matter had become public knowledge and a
source of humour in popular newspapers.

Mr Edwardes has not favoured me with the courtesy of a
reply to my various letters of protest (indeed he appears to
have gone to ground - as well he might!) and it now seems
certain that he intends to appropriate my idea without payment.

I think you will agree that in the circumstances punitive
damages would be awarded to me in the High Court.

The other matter is somewhat more trivial. As the enclosed
documents will show, I recently submitted four comical definitions
and a humorous poem to Esther Rantzen's excellent TV Show 'That's
Life'. I have chased up the BBC's accounts department, but so
far no money has been forthcoming and I judge that now is the time
to sue them.

I look forward to hearing that you can act for me with your
customary vigour in these two matters.

Yours sincerely,

Henry Root

Henry Root.

Eric Levine Keith Fletcher Kevin Gillon Tilly Halliwell John Wood Caroline Janzen

63 LINCOLN'S INN FIELDS LONDON WC2A 3LW TELEPHONE 01-405 7855
TELEX 28988 TELEGRAMS ELJURIS LONDON

24th April 1979

H. Root, Esq.,
139 Elm Park Mansions,
Park Walk,
London SW 10

Dear Mr. Root,

I thank you for your letter of 17th April addressed
to Mr. Levine.

Mr. Levine is presently abroad and will be travelling
significantly over the next several weeks. I will of course
pass your letter to him when he is next in London. It may
be that you would wish to pass your letters to somebody who
will have a greater amount of time available to deal with the
matter.

Yours sincerely,

KAY TALBOT
Secretary to:
ERIC LEVINE

/KAT

Ms Kay Talbot,
Eric Levine & Co,
63 Lincoln's Inn Fields,
London, W.C.2.

139 Elm Park Mansions
Park Walk
London, S.W.10.

26th April 1979.

Dear Ms Talbot,

Thank you for your letter of 24th April with regard to the matter between British Leyland and myself.

I'm sorry to hear that Mr Levine is abroad and travelling 'significantly' over the next several weeks. Nothing amiss, I hope?

I'm particularly eager to prosecute this bit of litigation with all due haste and since I have heard such excellent things about your firm I am wondering whether one of the other partners might handle the dodge for me?

I see the name of Mr Keith Fletcher at the top of your writing paper. Would this by any chance be the Keith Fletcher (known affectionately to his team-mates as 'The Gnome') who skippers Essex at cricket? If so, I would be more than happy for him to handle the caper for me. He's a wily skipper who reads the game well and although I've seen him drop a couple of sitters in the slips in my time, I'm sure he won't be a butter-fingers with this one!

It so happens that I'll be in your part of the world next Friday 4th May, so unless I hear that it would be inconvenient I'll drop by at 12.30 for an initial conference with 'The Gnome'.

Yours sincerely,

Henry Root

Henry Root.

ERIC LEVINE & CO.

Eric Levine Keith Fletcher Kevin Gillon Tilly Halliwell John Wood Caroline Janzen

63 LINCOLN S INN FIELDS LONDON WC 2 A 3LW TELEPHONE 01-405 7855
TELEX 28988 TELEGRAMS ELIURIS LONDON

27th April 1979

H. Root, Esq.,
139 Elm Park Mansions,
Park Walk,
London SW 10

Dear Mr. Root,

I thank you for your letter of 26th April the content of which together with your earlier letter I have now had the opportunity of discussing with Mr. Levine.

Mr. Levine regrets that he is not able to act for you in this matter since it is not the type of matter that the firm deals with.

Yours sincerely,

KAY TALBOT
Secretary to:
ERIC LEVINE

139 Elm Park Mansions
Park Walk
London, S.W.10.

Mr 'Larry' Lamb,
The Sun,
30 Bouverie Street,
London, E.C.4.   31st March 1979.

Dear Mr Lamb,

        As a 'Sun' reader for many years (Mrs Root chaffs me that I
only take it for the pretty girls - but what's wrong with a pretty
girl!!?), may I say how shocked I was this morning to read the following story on your TV page?

        'Fun-loving Ian McShane could not resist the temptation to
send-up the Last Supper while 'Jesus of Nazareth' was being filmed.
McShane, 36, who plays Judas, says: "I had to sneak out of the door
with evil in my heart, to betray Christ. I sneaked out all right - th
then I stuck my head back round the door and said: 'I have got it
right, haven't I? Five hake, two rock salmon, five plaice and twelve
chips?' They all fell about!" It was just one of the many zany
things that happened during the making of 'Jesus of Nazareth' (ITV,
Sunday 6.30) in Morocco.....'

        It's one thing for some prancing mime to act the goat at a
poignant moment in Our Lord's story; quite another for a family newspaper such as yours to report his oafish antics with apparent approval.

        Don't misunderstand me. I'm no 'Disgusting of Tunbridge Wells'.
I've knocked around the world and so has Mrs Root. We like a bit of
harmless fun as much as the next couple (Fred and Rita Snipe in 138).
Nudity (and yours is always tasteful) is all right in its place;
blasphemy, on the other hand, is below the belt.

        I look forward to receiving your explanation for this deplorable
lapse and to your confirmation that the journalist responsible, Chris
Kenworthy, has been relieved of his position.

        Yours sincerely,

        Henry Root

        Henry Root.

Copies to: The Press Council.
             Lord Grade.
             Mrs Whitehouse.
             Lord Goodman.
             Mary Kenny.

Lord Grade,
ATV,
17 Great Cumberland Place,
London, W.1.

139 Elm Park Mansions
Park Walk
London, S.W.10.

31st March 1979.

Dear Lord Grade,

Since I have always assumed that you are a religious man in the widest sense of the word (albeit of a different faith to that of myself, Mrs Root and Mary Kenny) as well as being a man with an eye for a profit (and what's wrong with that?), I thought you would be interested in the enclosed letter which I have sent this morning to Mr 'Larry' Lamb, Editor-in-Chief of Sun Newspapers.

I assume that you would not wish your fine and always tasteful TV film 'Jesus of Nazareth' to be the occasion of cheap jokes by unthinking actors.

Yours sincerely,

Henry Root

Henry Root.

P.S. When are we to have the pleasure of Miss Shirley McLaine on our screens again? Now there's a <u>thinking</u> actress, who appeals to the whole family.

THE Sun

NEWS GROUP NEWSPAPERS LTD
A Subsidiary of News International Ltd

Registered No. 679215 England
Telex Sunnews 267827
Telephone 01-353 3030
EDITOR'S OFFICE

Registered Office:

30 Bouverie Street, Fleet Street, London, EC4Y 8DE.

April 3rd, 1979.

AL/MD

Henry Root, Esq.,
139, Elm Park Mansions,
Park Walk,
London, SW10.

Dear MR Root —

Thank you for your letter.

I am sorry you were offended by the McShane story. It is never any part of our purpose to offend.

I agree, on reflection, that the story may well strike some people as being in dubious taste. But we didn't invent it, nor did we necessarily approve. We just reported.

And I really don't think I can sack Mr. Kenworthy for what was, at worst, a relatively minor misjudgment.

Now that would be below the belt!

With best wishes,

Yours sincerely,

Larry Lamb,
EDITOR.

**Associated
Communications
Corporation
Limited**

ATV House
17 Great Cumberland Place
London W1A 1AG
telephone 01-262 8040
cables and telegrams
Ayteevee London W1
telex 23762

Directors
Lord Grade Chairman
  and Chief Executive
Jack Gill CBE Deputy Chairman
  and Deputy Chief Executive
Louis Benjamin Deputy Chairman
Sir Max Aitken Bt DSO DFC
E S Birk
Norman Collins
Alexander Jarratt CB
Victor Matthews
Lord Willsborough

From the office of Lord Grade

11th April, 1979.

Dear Mr. Root,

Thank you for your note of
March 31st with the attached correspondence.

I know that all the actors in
our "JESUS OF NAZARETH" production worked
extremely hard over a long period and many
of them said afterwards how being involved
in the production helped to renew their
faith in their particular religious beliefs.
Young actors working in difficult
circumstances may be forgiven moments of
high spirits and I feel the newspapers may
have exaggerated this out of all proportion.

I am sorry if you found the
particular incident disturbing, but knowing
Ian McShane, I am confident that this has
been related out of context.

Yours sincerely,

(Lord Grade)

Mr. Henry Root

Registered Office : ATV House 17 Great Cumberland Place London W1A 1AG
Registered in England No. 544144

139 Elm Park Mansions
Park Walk
London, S.W.10.

Her Majesty the Queen (and Duke of Normandy!)
Buckingham Palace,
London, S.W.1.

9th April 1979.

Your Majesty,

With the greatest respect, I take leave to surmise that as
a mother you will be no less concerned than Mrs Root is about this
once great nation's collapse in terms of moral leadership.

I appreciate that under the constitution you cannot poke
your nose into things too directly, but I do have a small suggestion to make.

You're always opening things: hospitals, schools, theatres,
factories, fly-overs, play-grounds etc.

Why don't you <u>close</u> a few things?

I have in mind such blemishes on the face of our society as
The National Liberal Club, BBC 2, Soho's 'foreign' cinemas and
so-called massage parlours, the National Council for Civil Lib-
erties, subversive periodicals such as 'The New Statesman' and
'Time Out', which are devoted to the undermining of family life
and our British institutions, and the new white tile universities,
which see it as their function to stuff the impressionable young
students with half-baked left-wing notions.

With great respect, Ma'am, I shouldn't have to remind you
how gratified your late grandmother, Queen Victoria, would have
been to see you give the nation a moral lead in these matters.

Support Mrs Thatcher!

Royalists demand the return of the rope!

Your humble subject,

Henry Root

Henry Root.

139 Elm Park Mansions
Park Walk
London, S.W.10.

Miss Angela Rippon,
BBC News,   9th April 1979.
Television Centre,
London, W.12.

Dear Miss Rippon,
        I and many millions of your admirers must have been disappointed
to read in the paper yesterday that you plan to sue the Mirror Group
for calling you the 'Iron Maiden'.
        What is insulting or damaging about such a cognomen? Is not
our future Leader, Mrs Thatcher, known as 'The Iron Lady'? What
could be a greater honour than to be associated in the public con-
sciousness with such a fine woman?
        I gather that you think the name suggests that you are some
sort of lemon-faced puritan. What's wrong with that? Surely a lib-
erated woman such as yourself doesn't want to be thought of as a
scatter-brained sex-symbol, subjected each night to the insulting
stares of frustrated men who think women are for one thing only?
Your admirers like you just the way you are.
        Could you possibly send me a photograph of Anna Ford? I'd
write to her myself, but as I'm already writing to you it seems
silly to waste a stamp.

        Yours sincerely,

        Henry Root

        Henry Root.

P.S. In case you intend to pursue your mistaken action for damages,
I enclose a pound to help with the costs. I don't approve of what
you are doing, but I'd like to support you all the same. I also
enclose the postage for Anna Ford's photograph. Thank you.

BRITISH BROADCASTING CORPORATION
TELEVISION CENTRE WOOD LANE LONDON W12 7RJ
TELEPHONE 01-743 8000   TELEX: 265781
TELEGRAMS AND CABLES: TELECASTS LONDON TELEX

Dear Mr Post

What an extraordinary
letter!

I have sued the Mirror
Group – not for calling me an "Iron
maiden" but for a 2 page article
in Reveille which contained numerous
accusations and slanderous comments.

You are obviously a man
of intelligence – why then reach a
conclusion from a paraphrased note
when you would have been able
to make an informed observation
(and an accurate one) by reading
the full article.

As I have won the case
I have no costs, so I return
your contribution with thanks.
Yours sincerely

Angela Rippon.

139 Elm Park Mansions
Park Walk
London, S.W.10.

The Lucie Clayton Model Agency,
168 Brompton Road,
London, S.W.1.   9th April 1979.

Dear Sir or Madame,

        Once a year the officers and men of the Rifle Brigade meet
to discuss old times in the course of a knees-up. Yours truly is
the Organising Secretary of this year's get-together which is to
be held in a private suite at the Savoy Hotel on Friday 25th May.

        I'd like you to supply the cabaret. What we have in mind
are a dozen or so 'models' to jump out of a cake and 'mingle' with
the guests.

        I naturally don't want to be too explicit in a letter, but
perhaps I should emphasise that the 'models' should be top types
and would be expected to 'go a bit', if you follow me.

        We would be prepared to pay each girl a minimum of £100 for
the evening's work, and no girl would be required to 'go with' more
than six officers or two men.

        I look forward to doing business with you.

        Yours sincerely,

        Henry Root

        Henry Root.

168 Brompton Road London SW3 1HW   01-581 0024

LUCIE CLAYTON

4th May 1979

Henry Root Esq
139 Elm Park Mansions
LONDON SW10

Dear Mr Root

Neither the Savoy Hotel, nor the adjutant
of your former regiment, confirm your state-
ment about the 25th May and certainly you
are writing to the wrong agency. I have,
however, been on to the Provost-Marshal's
department who will be sending some men
to see what it is that you really need.

Yours sincerely

S Neill
REGISTRAR

50
Years

LUCIE CLAYTON LIMITED   FOUNDED 1928

Directors: Lucie Clayton   Ann Bridger   Cecilia Lumley   Leslie Kark M.A. Oxon., F.R.S.A. Chairman

The Registrar,
Lucie Clayton, Ltd,
168 Brompton Road,
London, S.W.3.

139 Elm Park Mansions
Park Walk
London, S.W.10.

5th May 1979.

Dear Miss Neill,
    I don't understand. It was the Provost Marshal who recommended
you in the first place.
    Yours sincerely,

Henry Root.

139 Elm Park Mansions
Park Walk
London, S.W.10.

Miss Mary Kenny,
The Sunday Telegraph,
Fleet Street,
London, E.C.4.

12th April 1979.

Dear Miss Kenny,

        May I say how much I appreciate your articles in 'The Sunday
Telegraph' with their emphasis on the need at this time to affirm
the importance of family life?

        They are an inspiration in these days of sexual pleasure off
the leash.

        I wonder if I could ask your advice on a matter of dispute
between Mrs Root and myself? I hold that oral contraception is
only necessary if you indulge in oral sex, but Mrs Root argues
otherwise.

        I would stress that this has nothing to do with the personal
life of myself and Mrs Root. I did my duty by her many years ago -
we have two grand youngsters, Doreen (19) and Henry Jr (15) - and
of course oral sex never came into it in those days. No, the
matter has arisen because Doreen plans to go on holiday this
summer with a male student from Essex University. Mrs Root thinks
she should have a word in her ear about 'precautions', however
unpleasant this may be for both of them.

        I write to you because you seem like a valid, caring person.
I expect you get literally millions of letters a week from confused
ordinary folk, so I enclose the return postage to facilitate the
convenience of your advice.

        I read somewhere that you're writing a book about the meaning
of God. That's one to look forward to! Well done!

        Yours for the Family!

        Henry Root

        Henry Root.

139 Elm Park Mansions
Park Walk
London, S.W.10.

The London Theatre Organiser,
British Actors Equity,
8 Harley Street,
London, W.1.

17th April 1979.

Dear Sir or Madam,

This is to inform you that Root Touring Productions Ltd will
be holding open auditions for its next attraction – 'The English
Way of Doing Things' by Henry Root – on the evening of Tuesday 24th
April, at 9.30 at the above address.

Artistes will be required to disrobe frontally and show themselves available in all positions to undertake acts of simulated
intercourse for the benefit of myself (choreographer) and Mr and
Mrs Snipe (investors) who live next-door.

It is my understanding that an Official Equity Observer likes
to be present at such times, and who shall blame him? Nice work
if you can get it!

I look forward to meeting your representative on 24th April
at 9.30.

Yours for Family Entertainment!

Henry Root

Henry Root.

T

889077 PO FD G
299992 PO TS G

J172 1734 LONDON T SW 18

HENRY ROOT 139 ELM PARK MANSIONS PARK WALK
LONDONSW10

CONTACT EQUITY URGENT .
MIKE CHATTIN OR CATHY ALLEN

139 10 .

889077 PO FD G
299992 PO TS G

139 Elm Park Mansions
Park Walk
London, S.W.10.

Sir Aubrey Melford Stevenson,
Truncheons,
Winchelsea,
East Sussex.   16th April 1979.

M'Lud,

    So - this is a sad day for Law and Order! A sad day too
for the ordinary man in the street who asks nothing more of life
than that his women-folk should be able to go about their business without having first to be rigged out with an 'Anti-Rape
System' or 'Personal Protection Kit' now being marketted by the
excellent firm of Personal Hazard Protection Ltd, of 69 Silver-
town Way, London E.16 (Tel No 01-476-5648, should you want to
give them a ring.)

    Equally, it's a day of celebration for softies, sapphists,
kid-glove pansies, liberals and sodomites.

    Here's a pound. Not much, I'm afraid, but if ordinary folk
everywhere gave a pound to great public servants on their retirement they wouldn't be reduced, like that fine man Sir Robert
Mark, to driving breakdown vans for the AA, selling life assurance
door-to-door, working as masseurs in so-called 'health farms' and,
most humiliating of all, perhaps, appearing in deodorant ads on TV.

    God bless you, M'Lud!

    Yours for Law and Order!

    Henry Root

    Henry Root.

Truncheons
Winchelsea
Sussex

18th April 1979

Dear Mr Rooke

Thank you so much for your
letter and all the kind things you
say. I much appreciate them

As to the pound you so generously
sent I have thought it right
to hand it over to the Sussex Police
Welfare fund which I know
does valuable work in helping
gallant Police and their families
when they need it. I am sure
you will agree with this course
as I am precluded from receiving
personal gifts

I enclose the receipt. You may
get a further acknowledgment from
the Headquarters

Yours v. sincerely
Melford Stevenson

139 Elm Park Mansions
Park Walk
London, S.W.10.

Mr Richard Ryder,
Conservative Party H.Q.,
32 Smith Square,
London, S.W.1.   17th April 1979.

Dear Ryder,

Sorry I haven't been in touch since 29th March! I've been up to my eyebrows in it. I expect you have too. I'm now catching up with my correspondence and am resolved not to fall so badly behind again. Please convey my apologies to Mrs Thatcher.

I am addressing myself to you and have marked this letter 'Private and Confidential' since I want to touch on a rather delicate matter concerning our Leader's health and one which I judge to be best discussed between men. (No doubt Mrs Thatcher, in her courageous way, would deny that anything was wrong.)

The fact is I read in my paper the other day that a Dr Patrick Cosgrave is a constant and close attendant on her. Wishing to discover the precise nature of her complaint, I took advantage of a consultation with my own doctor (dont worry! - just my annual blood pressure read-out) to persuade him to check out Dr Cosgrave's speciality in the BMA register of practitioners.

Imagine our sense of mystification when we found no one of this name qualified to practise medicine in the British Isles!

Eventually my doctor surmised that Dr Cosgrave must be a chiropodist, explaining that practitioners of this trade often attach the prefix 'Dr' to their names, though not officially encouraged so to do.

Does our Leader suffer from corns? These can be the very devil, as Mrs Root would be the first to tell you. With so many electoral walk-abouts to do, it seems to me a tantamount priority that Mrs Thatcher should rest up as much as possible and eschew tight shoes.

Mrs Root was once bed-ridden for three weeks. No great hardship for the country in her case, but the people can ill-afford Mrs Thatcher's absence from the centre of things for a like period.

Here's a pound. Persuade our Leader to take it easy. I'll leave this to you.

Bring back the rope!

Yours sincerely,

Henry Root.

Henry Root.

From

The Rt. Hon. Mrs Margaret Thatcher

Conservative & Unionist Central Office, 32 Smith Square, Westminster SW1P 3HH

18th April 1979

Dear Mr Root,

Thank you very much for your letter of 17th April.

Dr Cosgrave has, I believe, a PhD. This is as you know an academic qualification not a medical one. Dr Cosgrave has never claimed to be a doctor of medicine.

Finally thank you for your very kind contribution. It is greatly appreciated.

With best wishes,

Yrs Sincerely,

Richard Ryder
Private Office

H Root Esq

139 Elm Park Mansions
Park Walk
London, S.W.10.

Dr Dawid de Villiers,
The South African Embassy,   17th April 1979.
South Africa House,
London, W.C.2.

Your Excellency!
    May I say what a rare pleasure it is to have a running scrum-
half at the Court of St James? I don't usually agree with dragging
sport into politics, but I'm happy to make an exception in your case.
    I saw you play a few times in your youth, Sir, and by jingo you
could go a bit! I know what goes on in those scrummages unperceived
by the naked eye in the stands and I never saw you elbow an opponent
in the eye or squeeze a fellow's under-parts. You were a gentleman
scrum-half, Sir.
    Because of the internal difficulties of your great country
(which Mrs Root and I had the great pleasure of visiting a year or
two ago) you'll run into a bit of flack over here from ignorant
elements in our society: professional liberals who, at a safe dis-
tance, like to protest at the robust methods by which your hard-
pressed security police uphold the law. I don't have to tell you
not to pay any attention. Peter so-called Hain has no constituency.
What does he know of your country's internal difficulties? It's an
intolerable impertinence, in my opinion, for the citizens of one
country to criticise the customs of another, and I hope very much
that, in the course of your stay with us, you'll be outspoken in your
own criticisms of anyone in this country who holds an opposing view.
    Could you oblige with a photograph? As a philosopher and a
diplomat you may disapprove of personality cults, but I'm trying to
persuade my boy Henry Jr (15) that soccer's a girl's game and I
reckon that a photo of a fine looking man like you in his room might
do the trick.
    Up the Springboks!
    We haven't forgotten Rorke's Drift even if the Zulus have!
    Yours Against Interfering in the Internal Affairs of Another
Country!

Henry Root

Henry Root.

South African Embassy

25 April 1979

LONDON   WC2N   5DP

Mr Henry Root
139 Elm Park Mansions
Park Walk
LONDON SW 10

Dear Mr Root

Thank you very much for your friendly letter and warm words of welcome.   Your very kind remarks about me are sincerely appreciated.

I am delighted to hear that you have visited South Africa and have gained a favourable impression of our country.   We do not ignore the fact that we have pressing problems.   However these problems are much more complicated than what most critics are prepared to acknowledge.   I am convinced that the peoples of South Africa are in the best position to solve their own problems and will do so, given the opportunity.   The majority of the people in South Africa, black and white, are dedicated to resolve the problems in a peaceful and evolutionary way. Great strides have already been taken in that direction.

It gives me pleasure to oblige you in your request for a photo for Henry.

Yours sincerely

Dr D J de Villiers
Ambassador

Best wishes Henry from Dawie de Villiers

139 Elm Park Mansions
Park Walk
London, S.W.10.

Nicholas Scott MP,
Chelsea Conservative Party,
1a Chelsea Manor Street,
London, S.W.1.   17th April 1979.

Dear Mr Scott,

Don't get me wrong - I'm a Tory, always have been, always will
be. However, before casting my vote for you in the coming election
I would like to be reassured on one point.

Are you, like our Leader Mrs Thatcher, committed to the re-
introduction of selective hanging? If you are, I'm afraid I will
be unable, as a matter of conscience, to vote for you.

The concept's nonsense, and the one plank in her platform on
which I and Mrs Thatcher (with whom I have been in close touch
throughout the campaign) are unable to agree.

Was the Battle of Britain won by shooting down Jerry selectively? I should say not! We pranged the buggers willy-nilly! Now
that we are engaged in another, and no less desperate, Battle of
Britain we can be certain of one thing: we won't defeat the enemy
in our midst - terrorists, weirdos and extremists under the bed - by
hanging them selectively. We've got to hang the lot!

I look forward to hearing that you agree with me on this vital
issue.

Here's a pound.

Yours for Law and Order!

Henry Root

Henry Root.

Nicholas Scott
Conservative

General Election
3rd May 1979

Chelsea
Campaign Headquarters
1a Chelsea Manor Street,
London, S.W.3.
Tel: 352 0102

Election Agent: R. A. Rogerson

2ᴜ April 1979

Dᴇᴀʀ Mr Root

Thank you very much indeed for your
contribution to the Fighting Fund.

Like you, I do not approve of selective
hanging!

Yours sincerely

Nicholas Scott

Henry Root Esq,
139 Elm Park Mansions,
Park Walk, London S.W.10

Published by R. A. Rogerson, 1a Chelsea Manor Street, London, S.W.3   Printed by J. G. Bryson, (Printer) Ltd., 156/164 High Road, N.2

139 Elm Park Mansions
Park Walk
London, S.W.10.

Nicholas Scott MP,
1a Chelsea Manor Street,   26th April 1979.
London, S.W.3.

Dear Mr Scott,
        Thank you for your letter of 20th April, but you will forgive
me if I say your answer to my question on selective hanging was somewhat evasive (typical of a politician!)

        'Like you, I do not approve of selective hanging', you write.
You will agree that this is rather ambiguous to say the least. It
might mean that you are against all hanging (though I can scarcely
bring myself to believe this of a Tory) or it might mean that, like
me, you think everyone should be hanged.

        It's not in my nature to be a bore, and I must apologise for
being so persistent on this point. It's most important to me, however to get an unambiguous reply before voting for you on 3rd May.

        Here's another pound!

        Up our Leader!

        Yours Against Bennery Under the Bed,

        Henry Root

        Henry Root.

P.S. Talking about beds, may I say - without straying into impertinence, I hope - that I trust all is now well between you and Mrs
Scott? It's always sad when the private lives of our public servants
are at sixes and sevens, and it must be said that Tories tend to be
rather weak-willed and easily-led in these matters.

General Election
3rd May 1979

Chelsea
Campaign Headquarters
1a Chelsea Manor Street,
London, S.W.3.
Tel: 352 0102

Election Agent: R. A. Rogerson

Nicholas Scott
Conservative

2b April 1979

Dear Mr Root

Thank you for your further contribution.

I am sorry you found my reaction ambiguous but
I really did think my views on this matter were
well known in the constituency.

I share the views of those of my colleagues in
the Tory Party who are opposed to the principle
of capital punishment.   This is not to say I
am against convicted terrorists spending the
rest of their natural lives in gaol, but I do
not accept that the threat of hanging is a
deterrent to murder and indeed as far as terrorists
are concerned my fear is that it could be tragically
counter-productive.

Thank you for the kind thoughts behind your
personal enquiry.   I do not want to be evasive,
but just at this special moment in time I can
only reassure you that all is well.

Yours sincerely

Henry Root Esq.

139 Elm Park Mansions
Park Walk
London, S.W.IO.

Richard Ryder Esq,
Conservative Central Office,
32 Smith Square,
London, S.W.I.   26th April I979.

Dear Ryder,

        Many thanks for your letter of I8th April.

        It was a great relief to discover that Dr Cosgrave is not,
after all, a chiropodist and indeed that our Leader is in perfect
health.

        May I say how delighted I was to read in yesterday's 'Evening
Standard' that our Leader doesn't 'wish to see the death penalty
used a very great deal'. This dispels the popular idea that she
intends to be personally present at all hangings. This seems to me
to be the right attitude. She should only attend the more important
ones.

        May I also take this opportunity of saying how pleased I was
to read in 'The Sun' today that she has written personally to Mrs
Whitehouse, giving that good lady her personal guarantee that she
will crack down hard on the porno merchants when she comes to power.
I see that young Mr Steel characteristically failed to join in the
dialogue with Mrs Whitehouse on this vital topic. The boy has no
feel for the relevant issues. Mrs Thatcher understands that our
leaders ignore Mrs Whitehouse at their peril. She doesn't have to
be reminded of what happened to those easily-led light-weights, me
noble Lords Lambton and Jellicoe. (You'll notice that I deliber-
ately failed to mention Mr Profumo. It's high time, in my opinion,
that the poor man should be allowed to forget that he slept with a
tart, endangered the security of his country and lied to the House
of Commons.)

        Here's a pound. Use it to crack down on the porno barons.

        Bring back the rope!

        Your Man on the Door-Step!

        Henry Root

        Henry Root.

P.S. Henry Root's no tell-tale but I think you ought to know that
I've had a most unsatisfactory letter from Nicholas Scott (my local
MP) on the subject of selective hanging. Is it too late to put up
another candidate in this area?

Copy to Nicholas Scott MP.

From

The Rt. Hon. Mrs Margaret Thatcher

Conservative & Unionist Central Office, 32 Smith Square, Westminster SW1P 3HH

1st May 1979

Dear Mr Root,

Thank you very much for your kind
letter of 26th April. I am most
grateful to you for sending £1
towards our Campaign Fund. It is
much appreciated.

With best wishes.

Yours sincerely,

Richard Ryder
Private Office

Henry Root Esq

Duke Hussey,
The Times,
New Printing House Square,
Gray's Inn Road,
London, W.C.1.

139 Elm Park Mansions
Park Walk
London, S.W.10.

18th April 1979.

Your Grace,

I want you to know that Mrs Root and I were inspired by your
performance on 'The News' last night.

Never go down to the Unions! That's not the way to beat the
extremists under the bed.

"We plan to change the philosophy of Fleet Street," you said.

Well, I don't know much about philosophy (I left school at sixteen) but I do know I didn't get to the top in fish by truckling to
militants.

I'm a 'Telegraph' man myself, but here's a pound. Not much, but
if every 'Telegraph' reader sent you a pound the fight against the
trouble-makers would be funded for another month.

Good luck!

Never give in!

Yours sincerely,

Henry Root

Henry Root.

TIMES NEWSPAPERS LIMITED

Registered office: P.O. Box no. 7, New Printing House Square,
Gray's Inn Road, London WC1X 8EZ
Telephone 01-837 1234 Telex 264971 Registered no. 894646 England

April 23rd, 1979

Henry Root, Esq.
139 Elm Park Mansions
Park Walk
London, SW10

Dear Mr. Root,

Thank you so much for your letter of
April 18th, and particularly for the
£1 note which I am giving to our
Widows and Orphans Fund.

We are fighting as hard as we can
and we do not intend to give in.

With all good wishes.

Yours sincerely,

M.J. Hussey
Chief Executive and
Managing Director

139 Elm Park Mansions
Park Walk
London, S.W.10.

C.James Anderton Q.P.M., F.B.I.M.
Chester House,
Boyer Street,
Manchester MI6 ORE.   19th April 1979.

Dear Chief Constable,

I am so sorry not to have replied sooner to your letter
of 27th March. Mrs Root and I are naturally disappointed that
you're unable to address a meeting of 'The Ordinary Folk Against
Porn Society', but we quite understand that you're flat to the
boards chasing porno merchants off your patch. Well done!

Don't worry about this, because I've had an idea! We'll
come to you!

Would Tuesday 8th May be convenient? If so we'll muster in
your office at, say, four pm on that day. There'll just be a
handfull of us: myself and Mrs Root, Major Dewdrop, Dr Littlewinkle and his good lady, the Snipes (Fred and Rita) together
with their youngsters, Molly (17) and Bruce (19) and the Smithsons.

We wouldn't want you to go to any trouble on our behalf,
so please don't lay on much of a show. A cup of tea (Indian
please) and some rock cakes would be just fine. I certainly don't
wany to eat into funds that would be better employed putting
pimps in the pokey so I enclose a pound to cover the cost of
any hospitality you arrange.

Bring back the rope!
Your pal in the soft south!

Henry Root

Henry Root.

PS. Please let me know if you can't make it on the arranged date.
I'd hate to run into your office with my party only to find you'd
sugared off early to play golf with the Lord Mayor!

C James Anderton Q.P.M., F.B.I.M.
Chief Constable

Chief Constable's Office
P O Box 22 (S.West PDO)
Chester House
Boyer Street
Manchester M16 0RE
Telephone 061-872 5050

23rd April 1979.

Dear Mr. Root,

I have your letter of 19th April but regret I
am not available to meet you as you suggest on Tuesday, 8th May.
I am sorry about this.

I doubt if it will be possible for me to meet you
and your friends under such arrangements as my busy professional
life makes it virtually impossible for me to guarantee such
relatively informal contacts. I hope you will understand.

I am returning the £1.00 note you forwarded with
your letter.

Yours sincerely,

Chief Constable.

H.Root, Esq.,
139 Elm Park Mansions,
Park Walk,
London.S.W.10.

139 Elm Park Mansions
Park Walk
London, S.W.10.

Patrick Moore Esq,   19th April 1979.
Selsey,
West Sussex.

Dear Mr Moore,
        I was most interested to read in 'The Sun' yesterday about
the formation of The United Country Party.
        I'm not entirely sure that astrologers like yourself should
get mixed up in the real world of politics, but I like the sound
of your platform. (I hope it's a strong one! Let's face it, you're
no feather-weight!) At least you won't have to rely on the opinion
polls to tell you how you're doing. You'll be able to read it in
the stars! Not that I believe in any of this astrology nonsense.
We're very sceptical, we Capricorns!
        The aims of your party sound sensible. Abolish income tax,
clear the rubbish from the streets and crack down hard on the Welsh.
Just what the doctor ordered. I take it you're in favour of the
immediate re-introduction of hanging?
        I'd be most grateful if you could send me a copy of your
manifesto and also if you could let me know whether you're putting
up up a candidate in this constituency (Chelsea) for whom I can
vote.
        Yours for Law and Order!

        Henry Root

        Henry Root.

UNITED COUNTRY PARTY

VICE-CHAIRMAN & PARLIAMENTARY
CANDIDATE FOR CHICHESTER

CHAIRMAN:
Patrick Moore, OBE FRAS

Lt.-Col. E. A. L. Iremonger,
Durley, Sidlesham, Sussex.

TREASURER:
G. Gumersall,
93 Drift Road, Selsey.

SECRETARIAL ADDRESS:
39 West Street,
Selsey, Sussex
Tel: 024361-3668

BANKERS:
Lloyds Chichester.

Dear Mr. Root,

I hasten to stress that I am an astronomer, not an astrologer! -

Details of manifesto enclosed. Hanging is not on our manifesto, as we feel that this is a matter for everyone's own conscience. I am not a 'hanger' myself, but I believe most people are, and we'd prefer a free vote.

We are campaigning hard here.

All good wishes.

Sincerely

Patrick Moore

139 Elm Park Mansions
Park Walk
London, S.W.10.

Mr Nigel Dempsey,   19th April 1979.
The Daily Mail,
Carmelite House,
London, E.C.4.

Dear Dempsey,

May I say how much I have enjoyed your 'Diary' over the years? Some folk deride sycophantic gossip about one's social superiors as a lot of snobbish nonsense, but I am not of their number. Born, like you, without the advantages, I have acquired, like you, a healthy respect for my 'betters'. I have seen you described in some pseudo-intellectual magazine as having the morals of a cocktail waitress. So what? It happens to be the case that Mrs Root was a cocktail waitress when I met her and not once has she caused me to rue the day I plucked her off her bar-stool and made an honest woman of her.

I write to you now on a matter of some delicacy, but I'm sure I can rely on your discretion. The excellent firm of Jonathan Cape, of whom you may have heard, are shortly to publish my first novel, 'Day of Reckoning', and I am naturally eager that it should receive maximum media exposure.

I'm not some young idealist with his head in the literary clouds, but, like you, a down-to-earth businessman, and I haven't climbed to the top in fish without discovering that you don't get anywhere in life without - how shall I put this? - 'taking care of' a few influential people on the way. I expect you have found this out for yourself.

I now enclose a fiver on the understanding that you will write flatteringly about me when the book appears, linking my name with starlets and suggesting I'm intimate with Barry Sheene and his lady-friend 'Hotpants' Burbank. (I don't have to teach you your business.)

This is only the start. There's plenty more where this came from, so you be good to me and I'll see you're all right!

If you need some background information on me, please don't hestitate to let me know. I'm a very busy man but I could squeeze you in for an interview most mornings before 10am.

I look forward to reading the first item in your column!

Yours sincerely,

Henry Root

Henry Root.

139 Elm Park Mansions
Park Walk
London, S.W.10.

19th April 1979.

Jonathan Cape Esq,
Jonathan Cape Ltd,
30 Bedford Square,
London, W.C.1.

Dear Cape,   DAY OF RECKONING by HENRY ROOT.

I'm told you're always on the alert for solid yarns with no
unnecessary thrills, so I am now enclosing the synopsis of my
recently completed first novel as above.

Let me say at the outset that the 'property' comes to you
with certain advantages. For the right return on capital outlay,
I'm prepared to help with the financing of the caper (mainly to
ensure maximum media exposure - your people couldn't get a plug
for a bath, I'm told!) and I have taken the precaution of 'fixing'
certain journalists and literary editors. Nigel Dempsey of 'The
Daily Mail', for instance, is 'in my pocket'.

An additional advantage is that I shape up brand new in
public, come across well on camera (or so I was told after being
interviewed on a street-corner by Esther Rantzen on the hilarious
topic of, as she put it, 'getting your leg over the Mrs of a Saturday night') and I'm fully available with matching luggage to
undertake 'exploitation' tours - though not of Turkey, Greece or
Scandinavia.

Before I accept your offer, I should warn you that from a
business point of view I didn't just fall off a turnip truck. I'm
looking for a heavy advance as a guarantee that you aren't just
messing me about. I've heard of too many young writers for whom
an offer from a publisher turned out to be a stepping-stone to
obscurity.

Let's go!

Yours sincerely,

Henry Root

Henry Root.

Enc: Synopsis of DAY OF RECKONING by HENRY ROOT.

DAY OF RECKONING
By
HENRY ROOT.

Synopsis.

Bronzed, attractive, amazingly fit, 45-year-old Harry Toor, Chairman and Managing Director of Harry Toor Wet Fish Ltd, woke up in the sumptuously appointed bedroom of his luxury mansion in Maidenhead.

He stirred contentedly and, as was usual when he woke, he ran over in his mind his many blessings and possessions: his swimming-pool and tennis courts, his musical cocktail-cabinet and three-piece lounge-room suite in Victoria plum velvet with old-gold lurex edgings (a wedding present from his good mate and next-door neigh-bour, Michael Parkinson), his Rolls, his expense account trips to Paris, Geneva and New York, his yacht in Monte Carlo, his constant supply of willing 'personal secretaries' and, above all, his latest 'companion', the long-legged, full-bosomed 'starlet', Lorraine Pump-tit.

Suddenly he felt strangely ill at ease. Into his mind had come a vision of Barnsley and the back-street slum in which he'd been born and in which his 82-year-old dad and 80-year-old mum still lived. He hadn't visited them in over twnety years. Had it all been worthwhile, his ruthless drive to the top? Did he still know who he was? If he was to visit his old mum and dad now, sample once again his old mum's apple-pie and Yorkshire pudding, play darts with his old dad at the pub on the corner, would he still be able to talk to them, really communicate?

He thought of the little house in which he'd been born, of his old mum and dad, of the lads at the local pork-pie factory who had once been his mates, and of little Janet Gibbens with whom he'd had his first fumbling sexual experience in the back row of the Odeon and he thought:

"Stuff that lot. I'll stay put."

And he went contentedly back to sleep.

THE END.

Henry Root
139 Elm Park Mansions
Park Walk
London, S.W.7.
ALL RIGHTS RESERVED.

JONATHAN CAPE LIMITED
THIRTY BEDFORD SQUARE
LONDON W.C.1

Telephone 01-636 5764
Telex 299080
Answer CBCSER G

Telegrams
CAPAJON, LONDON WC1B 3EL

DB/ME

20th April, 1979

Mr Henry Root,
139 Elm Park Mansions,
Park Walk,
London. S.W.10.

Dear Mr Root,

Thank you for your letter of 19th April and synopsis. We regret
that we do not think it would be worth your while submitting your
typescript DAY OF RECKONING to us, as we do not feel that the
book would be entirely suited to our list.

Please find your synopsis enclosed.

Yours sincerely,

Debra Byron,
Editorial.

DIRECTORS: Tom Maschler Graham C. Greene Liz C...
Registered in England...

Daily Mail

TELEPHONE 01-353 6000
TELEGRAPH: DAILYMAIL LONDON-E.C.4

REGISTERED OFFICE
CARMELITE HOUSE,
LONDON, EC4Y OJA.
REGISTERED NO. 1160542 ENGLAND

GC/JEM

20 April, 1979

Mr. H. Root,
139 Elm Park Mansions,
Park Walk,
London, S.W.10.

Dear Mr. Root,

Thank you for your letter dated 19 April
which Mr. Dempster has passed to me.

It is not Mr. Dempster's habit, or that
of any other member of the Daily Mail
staff, to accept money, or anything else,
on the understanding that stories will
be written. In the circumstances I return
your £5.

Yours sincerely,

GORDON COWAN
Assistant Managing Editor

DAILY MAIL LTD. (Subsidiary of Associated Newspapers Group Ltd)
Directors: Hon. Vere Harmsworth (Chairman) R.M. Shields (Deputy Chairman) D English P Drover J.C. Johnston
J.A. Leese S.A. Martin B.A. Qiley J. Pearman D.R. Peck A.A. Robinson E.J. Winnington-Ingram

139 Elm Park Mansions
Park Walk
London, S.W.10.

Mr Gordon Cowan,
The Daily Mail,
Carmelite House,
London, E.C.4.   22nd April 1979.

Dear Mr Cowan,

        Thank you for your letter of 20th April in reply to my
letter of 19th April to Mr Nigel Dempster.

        Why can't he answer his own letters? I was addressing
myself to the monkey, not the organ-grinder. Is it the function
of an Assistant Managing Editor to act as secretary to the
paper's scandal writer? If so, what does the Managing Editor
do? The Snooker Correspondent's typing?

        Perhaps Mr Dempster will answer this letter. Or does
Mr English deal with your mail? It's all very confusing.

        Pending an explanation, I return the fiver.

        Yours sincerely,

        Henry Root

        Henry Root.

Daily Mail

TELEPHONE:- 01-353 6000
TELEGRAPH:- DAILYMAIL. LONDON-E.C.4.

REGISTERED OFFICE
CARMELITE HOUSE,
LONDON, EC4Y OJA.
REGISTERED NO. 1160542 ENGLAND

GC/JEM

2 May, 1979

Mr. H. Root,
139 Elm Park Mansions,
Park Walk,
London, S.W.10.

Dear Mr. Root,

Thank you for your further letter dated April 22.

Whatever you may think about newspaper production, or
whatevery you may expect, the only acknowledgment you will
receive in this matter is from me. Mr. Dempster quite
rightly brought it to my attention as the person in
charge of editorial administration.

You have now received the courtesy of two letters on the
matter and I consider this correspondence closed. I
return to you your money and reiterate that we do not
accept money from anyone on the understanding that
stories will be written about them.

Yours sincerely,

GORDON COWAN
Assistant Managing Editor

DAILY MAIL LTD. (Subsidiary of Associated Newspapers G
Directors: R.M.Shields (Chairman) D.English P.Grover J.C.Johnston
B.A.Olley J.Pearmain A.A.Robinson E.J.Winningto

139 Elm Park Mansions
Park Walk
London, S.W.10.

Mr Brian Clough,
'The Boss!',
Nottingham Forest F.C.,
Nottingham.

23rd March 1979.

Dear Mr Clough,

So you stuffed the Swiss! Magic! Mustard! You and the lads must be over the moon!

I was a bit disturbed by a pre-match report in my paper that you were thinking of buying their big striker, Sulser. The lad looks useful (you must have been as sick as a parrot when he stuck the ball in the back of the net to make it none one against you!) but where would this leave the boy Birtles? On top of which, is it possible for a foreign player to familiarise him-self with the English way of doing things? You know what I mean. I'm talking about being a credit to the game on and off the field. Short hair, smart appearance, train hard, no cussing or monkey-business in the changing-room and just one holiday a year with the wife and kiddies in Majorca.

Now, Henry Root's no snitch, but I think you ought to know that at half-time against the Grasshoppers, Archie Gemmill ('The Wee Man') blew his nose onto the pitch. Surely this isn't the Notts Forest way? I think you should remind your players that when they're on TV they are guests in our lounge-rooms and the last thing we want to see is them blowing their noses onto the lounge-room floor.

Anyway, here's a pound towards Sulser's fee. In spite of my reservations as expressed above, I recognise that you're the boss and that what you say goes.

You'll never walk alone!

Yours ever,

Henry Root

Henry Root.

139 Elm Park Mansions
Park Walk
London, S.W.10.

Mr Brian Clough,
'The Boss',
Nottingham Forest F.C.,
Nottingham.

23rd April 1979.

Dear Mr Clough,

Did you get my letter of 23rd March, enclosing a pound for the boy Sulser? Since you don't strike me as being the sort of man who'd pocket a pound without so much as a 'ta very much, lad', I assume my letter must have gone astray. In the circumstances, here's another pound. Let me know if this one doesn't arrive either.

Now - about the return with Cologne. I've got a daring suggestion to make. Drop the Big Man, Shilton! Let's face it, he failed to dominate 'the box' in the first leg and I ask myself whether he's got the bottle for the big occasion. Remember what happened in the World Cup against Poland? Perhaps in preferring Clemence, Mr Green-wood is turning out to be less stupid than he looks.

As for the two big centre-backs, well, one of them's got to go. Why don't you buy Toddy? I don't have to tell you of all people that he's still the most cultured No 6 in the world and I see he's now playing in the Everton Reserves, having had no less than sixteen of his majestic lapses in four minutes against West Bromwich last week. You could probably pick him up for a song or swop him for the wild-man Burnsy, who is not your sort of player. Some of us haven't forgotten how, against Arsenal last season, he saved a certain goal by knocking the opposing No 9 as cold as a stoat with an Army-surplus sandbag he'd taken with him onto the park. Effective, but not the Notts Forest way.

I'm glad to be able to report that at half-time in the first-leg against Cologne, Archie Gemmill ('The Wee Man') didn't blow his nose onto the pitch or do anything else to bring the game into disrepute. Possibly this was because he wasn't still on the field, having gone crook after a few minutes. I hope he's recovered now. He's a bonny wee fighter and you need him in the side.

Good luck in the return leg!

You're the Boss!

You'll never walk alone!

Your pal in the stands!

Henry Root

Henry Root.

Nottingham Forest Football Club

City Ground
Nottingham NG2 5FJ
Telephone 868236
Information Desk 860232
Pools Office 864808

Telegrams
Forestball Nottingham

Manager:
Brian Clough

Secretary/Treasurer:
Ken Smales

Founded 1865
Football League Division 1
Champions 1977/78
Football League Division 1
Runners Up 1966-67

Football League Cup Winners
1977/78

F.A. Cup Winners 1898 1959

Anglo Scottish Competition
Winners 1976-77

President G. N. Watson J.P
Chairman S. M. Dryden J.P
Vice-Chairman G. E. Macpherson J.P
Committee
H. W. Alcock F.C.A
B. J. Appleby Q.C
G. T. Thorpe
F. Reacher
T. C. Farr F.C.A
D. C. Pavis
D. J. Loch

Ref. BC/JMT

24th April, 1979.

Mr. H. Root,
139 Elm Park Mansions,
Park Walk,
London S.W.10.

Dear Mr. Root,

Thank you for your letters dated 23rd March and 23rd April, and I must apologise for not replying to you sooner, but having spent so much time with the players recently, due to playing four to five games per week, and I have had hardly any time to sit in the office and answer my correspondence. I have had to plough through a pile of over a one hundred letters to find your original correspondence, but I can assure you that you would have had a reply in due course.

I am returning the second pound note you sent me, but will put the original one into our "Sulser Fund"; and hope that you will not mind us using it for another transfer fee should say, Kevin Keegan, come onto the market first.

Once again, sorry for the delay, but I hope you understand my position.

Yours sincerely,

B. Clough,
Manager.

139 Elm Park Mansions
Park Walk
London, S.W.10.

Mrs Joan Pugh,
London Weekend Television Ltd,
London, S.E.1.   23rd April 1979.

Dear Mrs Pugh,

I am applying for the job of Programme Researcher in your new
'Minorities Unit', as advertised in this week's 'Spectator'.

Don't get me wrong. I've made my pile, I'm semi-retired and
I certainly don't need the work. But I'm glad to see your company's
leading the long over-due crackdown on the minorities in our society -
homosexuals, immigrants, drug addicts and young people - and I'd like
to support you. Quite frankly, after such unaffirmative shows as
'The London Programme' (in which, if Godfrey Hodgson isn't making
hearsay allegations against the Metropolitan CID, a sharp-nosed young
lady called Yvonne Roberts is poking up back alleys after prostitutes)
I'm agreeably surprised that you're at last taking a responsible line.
Worried about your licence being renewed? Nothing wrong with that.

Here are the facts of my life in a nut-shell:

Born 4th January 1935. Left school at 16 with one 'O' level
in geography (so I know my way around the world), but continued my
education at the University of Real Life, than which, you will agree,
there is none better.

From the age of 16 to 18 worked as a porter in Billingsgate
Fish Market. Gained invaluable experience of the English working
class's dislike of ethnic minorities and so-called intellectuals.
From 18 to 20 did my National Service in submarines under the legendary Captain 'Crap' Myers VC. Commissioned.

On being demobbed, started my own wet fish business. Worked
like a black (but paid myself rather better) and was able to sell
the business for a tidy sum in 1976. Now find myself with time on
my hands. Looking for new challenges with a societal bias.

Personal details: 5ft 8¾ins, 15 stone, English on both sides
of the family as far back as can be traced (1904). Expert shot.
Front upper denture due to boxing mishap sustained during National
Service. (17 fights, 2 convictions.) Married Muriel Root (née Potts)
in 1958. Two youngsters - Doreen (19) and Henry Jr (15.)

May I say how much I'm looking forward to joining your team and
to flushing out the ethnic woodworms from the fixtures and fittings
of our society.

Yours Against Minorities!

Henry Root

Henry Root.

P.S. I don't want to influence your decision one way or another,
but I think I ought to tell you that Mr Michael Grade is a personal
friend of mine, as the enclosed letter will show.

P.P.S. I'm a bit concerned about your address. Isn't S.E.1. rather
out of the picture media-wise? Can you assure me that, located as
you are on the wrong side of the river, you don't find yourselves
somewhat isolated from where it's happening? I don't want to be
stuck up some dead-end back-water.

LLWT

London Weekend Television

South Bank Television Centre, Kent House, Upper Ground, London SE1 9LT (Registered Office)
Telex: 918123. Cables: Weekendtel London SE1. PBX Telephone: 01-261 3434.

Direct Line: 01-261

29th March, 1979

Henry Root Esq.,
139 Elm Park Mansions,
Park Walk,
LONDON S.W.10.

Dear Mr. Root,

Thank you for your letter.

Yours sincerely,

MICHAEL GRADE
DIRECTOR OF PROGRAMMES

LLWT

London Weekend Television

South Bank Television Centre, Kent House, Upper Ground, London SE1 9LT (Registered Office)
Telex: 918123. Cables: Weekendtel London SE1. PBX Telephone: 01-261 3434.

Direct Line: 01-261 -3140

10th April, 1979

Henry Root, Esq.,
139, Elm Park Mansions,
Park Walk,
London SW10

Dear Mr. Root,

Thank you for your letter of the 9th May. I am sorry
that you have not received a reply to your application for the
London Minorities Unit vacancy, but I am afraid this may take
some time as we have had over 600 applications. You will however be notified if you are to be called for interview or not.

Thank you for your interest.

Yours sincerely,

Mrs. Joan Pugh,
Staff Officer

139 Elm Park Mansions
Park Walk
London, S.W.10.

The Rt Hon William Whitelaw,
Conservative Central Office,
32 Smith Square,
London, S.W.1.   24th April 1979.

Dear Mr Whitelaw,

Following the disgraceful and unprovoked attempt by left-wing
extremists to break up the perfectly lawful National Front meeting
in Southall last night, I was most relieved to hear you say on 'News
at Ten' that you would make no attempt as Home Secretary (which, God
willing, you soon will be) to ban further National Front rallies,
marches or meetings.

Don't misunderstand me - I'm no supporter of the Front. The pity
is that successive Governments, both Tory and Labour, have, by weak-
kneed policies on immigration, played into their hands. It remains
true, however, that a citizen has a basic human right to express his
views - however obnoxious these views may be. That's what we call
freedom of speech and it was reassuring, Sir, to hear you assert this
freedom on the News last night with all the considerable eloqence at
your command.

One thing bothers me, however. You will agree, I hope, that while
every citizen should have the right to express his opinions openly -
however unpleasant and prejudiced these opinion may be - this right
should not be granted to pornographers.

It is one thing to daub racist slogans in public places, quite
another for sweetshops and newsagents to openly display photographs
of naked ladies where kiddies can see them. You will agree, I think,
that our young folk are far more likely to be depraved and corrupted
by the latter than by the former.

Can I have your assurance, Sir, that as Home Secretary under Mrs
Thatcher, you will do nothing to impede the passage through Parliament
of Mr Hugh Rossi's sensible Obscene Displays Act, but that if, say,
The National Party of Pornographers and Pederasts tried to hold a
meeting in Southall you would stamp down on them with all your considerable weight?

I have two youngsters of my own, Sir, and I can assure you that
I would rather they exposed themselves to Mr Enoch Powell than that
they should be confronted in their local sweetshop by the naked bosoms
of some so-called 'topless model'.

Here's a pound. Use it to enforce law and order!

Yours for Freedom of Speech except for Pornographers!

Henry Root.

Copy to Mr Richard West.

PENRITH and THE BORDER CONSTITUENCY

PARLIAMENTARY ELECTION - 1979

CONSERVATIVE CANDIDATE
WILLIE WHITELAW

Election Agent:
N. B. DENT

CENTRAL COMMITTEE ROOMS,
31 CHISWICK STREET, CARLISLE
Telephone: Carlisle 21192

27th April, 1979

Dear Mr. Root,

Thank you very much for your kind donation to our Conservative Party.

I will always defend free speech in our country although I do equally vehemently oppose extremists who use violence utterly alien to our democratic tradition.

I can confirm that our Conservative Party will take action against pornography. Mr. Rossi's Bill revived legislation which our Government prepared in 1973 but which the present Government ignored on taking power.

Yours sincerely,

Annabel Dent

Dictated by Mr. Whitelaw and signed in his absence by his secretary.

Henry Root, Esq.,
139 Elm Park Mansions,
Park Walk,
London, S.W.10.

VOTE WHITELAW

**POLLING DAY
THURSDAY,
MAY 3rd**

Published by N. B. Dent, Election Agent, 31 Chiswick Street, Carlisle, and Printed by Reed's Ltd., King Street, Penrith.

139 Elm Park Mansions
Park Walk
London, S.W.10.

Mr Leslie Crowther,
c/o Thames Television Ltd,
306 Euston Road,
London, N.W.1.   26th April 1979.

Dear Leslie,

    Could you settle a dispute between me and Mrs Root? (You're
her favourite comedian - I can't think why! No, I'm only joking!)
Anyway, she holds that you're in your sixties, but I say that that's
impossible unless you've had your face lifted. But if you had had
your face lifted you wouldn't be able to smile all the time like
you do now. Your ears would drop off! I say you're only in your
late fifties. Could you settle this argument for us, once and for
all?

    Congratulations on your recent show on Thames! It was most
amusing - good clean family entertainment with no allusions to
matters appertaining to the water-works. (That's rare enough these
days, alas.)

    Here are a couple of wise-cracks you could use on your next
show. Just give me the credit. Say 'Additional wise-cracks by
Henry Root'. That would be okay.

1. Bob Monkhose. "You know, Dickie, it's not easy making millions
of people laugh".

    Dickie Henderson: "Sensible of you never to have tried, Bob!"

2. Question. "What's an innuendo?"

    Irish Literary Critic: "An Italian suppository!"

    Could you possibly oblige with a photo for Mrs Root? She'd
be really thrilled! I expect you get literally millions of letters
from ordinary folk like me, so I enclose the postage for your convenience.

    You're okay!

    Yours,

Henry Root

Henry Root.

Temple Court,
Corston,
Nr. Bath,
Avon.

Dear Henry,

      Many thanks for your delicious
letter which arrived in time for breakfast.

      Here is the photograph for
Mrs. Root - I could not get one of Bob
Monkhouse - which I hope she will like.

      Yours sincerely,

Good Luck !!

Leslie Crowther

Leslie Crowther.

Good Luck !!

Leslie Crowther

139 Elm Park Mansions
Park Walk
London, S.W.10.

General Zia-ut-Haq,   26th April 1979.
The Strong Man!,
The President's Office,
Islamabad,
Pakistan.

Mr President!
        In recent weeks you will have read unflattering reference
to yourself in our so-called liberal press. Pay no attention!
Most of us realise that a backward people such as yours needs,
and appreciates, the smack of firm government.
        We are not a backward people, of course, which makes our
sad National Decline in recent years all the harder for patriots
to stomach.
        Many take it as the final straw that in Kent - the garden
of England, I might remind you, Sir, - the county cricket team
is currently captained by a dusky character who rejoices in some
such unlikely name as Asif Iqbal!
        Happily for us, Margaret Thatcher - a strong man like your-
self - is about to come to power. As she stomps the country, in-
voking the glorious example of such great Englishman from our
island story as St Francis Drake and Sir Walter Pidgeon, the streets
ring with the sound of do-gooders breaking wind and taking to the
boats. Some will find a welcome, no doubt, in the licensed brothels
and drug-parlours of Holland and Denmark, but most will be blown
onto the rocks of obscurity by the hot wind of her rhetoric.
        Her first priority - and one which will greatly appeal to
you, Mr President - is the immediate restoration of capital punishment, not least for those who have committed murder. There's
a long way to go before Britain once again rules the world, of
course, but this is a step in the right direction, I think you'll
agree.
        Could you oblige with a photo, Mr President? It would have
pride of place, next to the late lamented Generalissiomo Franco, in
my gallery of great International Conservatives.
        You're all right!
        Yours respectfully,

        Henry Root

        Henry Root.

THE ISLAMIC REPUBLIC OF PAKISTAN

General M. Zia-ul-Haq

ISLAMABAD
57/2/CMLA
06 May 79

Henry Root, Esq
139 Elm Park Mansions
Park Walk
London, S.W. 10
U.K.

Dean Mr Root,

Thank you for your letter of 26 April 79.

I appreciate your thoughtfulness in writing to me to convey certain very pertinent views.

Enclosed is my photograph which you have requested. I have also signed it.

Wishing you all the best,

Yours sincerely,

General
(M. Zia-ul-Haq)

Mr Root, with my regards and very best wishes

                                                    139 Elm Park Mansions
                                                    Park Walk
                                                    London, S.W.10.

Ms Audrey Whiting,
Royal Correspondent!
The Sunday Mirror,
Holborn Circus,
London, E.C.1.   30th April 1979.

Dear Ms Whiting,

        I was deeply shocked to read your article in yesterday's
'Sunday Mirror' about the acute shortage of 'Royals' and the
consequent strain on Her Majesty the Queen.

        I have a suggestion to make. We now have Life Peers. Would
it not be sensible to apply this concept to the creation of Life
Royals?

        I have in mind folk of the utmost probity, folk who, like Her
Majesty, are above the rough and tumble of mere politics, folk who
have swum resolutely against the tide of declining morality over
the past years and have managed, lke Her Majesty, to affirm the
traditional values and family virtues in all they've done.

        I'm talking about people such as Group Captain Sir Douglas
'Hang 'em all' Bader, Miss Mary Kenny, Mr John Junor, Dr J.P.R.
Williams, Mr Bobby Charlton, Sir Richard Attenborough, Sir 'John'
Mills, Dame Ninette de Neagle, Miss Nanette Newman, Mr Laurie McMen-
emy ('The Big Man!'), Mary O'Hara the dancing nun from Glasgow (to
keep the Scots in their place) and Ms Val Doonican (ditto the Welsh.)

        You will notice that not all these people are from what might
be called 'the top drawer'. But the same could be said, let's face
it, of some of our present Royals. The criteria for being a Life
Royal should have nothing to do with 'class' as such. Life Royals,
like actual Royals, should be ordinary, but exceptional, folk up whom
lesser folk will naturally look but with whom they can relate.

        What do you think?

        Yours sincerely,

        Henry Root

        Henry Root.

Copies to: Her Majesty the Queen.
            Miss Mary Kenny.
            Mr John Junor.

139 Elm Park Mansions
Park Walk
London, S.W.10.

Her Majesty the Queen,
Buckingham Palace,
London, S.W.1.   30th April 1979.

Your Majesty,

      I enclose a copy of a letter I have sent today to Ms Audrey
Whiting, 'The Sunday Mirror's' Royal Authority.

      I was most shocked to read Ms Whiting's article about the
reluctance of certain members of your family to attend Royal Occasions
of the sort that Lord Delfont keeps arranging for you and I think
my concept of Life Royals might be the answer. (What a shame, incidentally, that I couldn't include Lord Delfont among my suggested
candidates for enroyalment. He would have been ideal, but by cre-
ating him a Life Peer, Sir Harold Wilson foolishly rendered him
unviable.)

      I was so sorry to read about the trouble you're having with
Princess Anne. My Doreen (19) is off the rails too, so I know what
it's like.

      Could you oblige with a photo, Ma'am? I'd be very honoured.

      Your humble subject,

Henry Root

      Henry Root.
Copy to Miss Mary Kenny.

FROM THE
EDITOR
OF THE
SUNDAY EXPRESS

FLEET STREET, LONDON
01-353 8000

1st May 1979

Dear Mr. Root,

Thank you very much for having sent me a copy of your letter to the Sunday Mirror.

I am greatly flattered by your nomination of me as a "Life Royal". But I very much doubt if the Royal Family would find me an acceptable substitute!

With all good wishes,

Yours sincerely,

JOHN JUNOR

Henry Root Esq.,
139, Elm Park Mansions,
Park Walk,
London. S.W.10.

BUCKINGHAM PALACE

10th May, 1979.

Dear Mr. Root,

     I am commanded by The Queen to write and thank you for your letter and enclosure, the contents of which have been noted.

     In answer to your request for a photograph of Her Majesty, I have to explain to you that owing to The Queen's rules in these matters, it is not possible to do as you ask.

     When I tell you of the many similar requests that Her Majesty receives, I feel sure you will understand the reason for these rules and that The Queen would not wish to break them for one and not for others.

Yours sincerely,

Susan Hussey.

Lady-in-Waiting

Henry Root Esq.,
139 Elm Park Mansions,
Park Walk,
London, S.W.1.

139 Elm Park Mansions
Park Walk
London, S.W.10.

The Prime Minister! (Mrs Margaret Thatcher!)
10 Downing Street,   4th May 1979.
London, S.W.1.

Dear Prime Minister!

Congratulations! We did it! What a day! History has been made!

Enough of that. As you said when you arrived at No 10 this afternoon: "There's work to be done."

That's right. It's straight down to business. (Don't worry! There'll be plenty of time later for women's work like measuring for new curtains!) We've got to form a Cabinet of hard-nosed men to prosecute our number 1 priority: the crackdown on the unions, the work-shy, law-breakers and homosexuals. I hope there won't be too many 'Oxbridge' men in our Cabinet. Dragged from the lecture-room into real life, they have trouble, in my experience, in discovering what day of the week it is. I'd like to make three suggestions:

1. For Home Secretary - Mrs Whitehouse. The self-appointed intellectuals sneer at her, but she's a mother like yourself. I read recently in 'The Sun' of how she visited you in your room at the House and how you showed each other pornographic pictures and knelt of the floor and prayed together. That was moving.

2. For Minister of Defence - Laurie McMenemy. As you may know he's the manager of Southampton FC at the moment, but he's got the shoulders to shine on a wider stage than the green turf of Wembley. Southampton have played in Europe, so he's had invaluable experience of 'kicking the foreigners into the stands'. I assume he's a Tory, but I'm writing to him on your behalf to check. I certainly never saw a Socialist with a back as straight as his.

3. For 'Our Man in Europe' - Paul Johnson. All right! All right! So they say he's a carrot-haired loony! So they call him Colonel 'Bonkers' Johnson! So what? Have they forgotten General Wolfe, the victor at Quebec? He was as mad as a hatter but he sent the Frogs packing! Johnson said to my father once:

"Root! You and I are old enough to remember a time when you could walk from one end of the Champs Elysées to the other without seeing a Frenchman! Those were the days!"

Johnson won't let you down, but watch out for the softies in the party. I don't much care for the look of Norman St John Stevas. My father taught me two things I've never forgotten.

"Mind this, son," he used to say. "Never spit in a man's face unless his moustache is on fire. And never trust a man who wears mauve underpants at tea-time."

I don't think we should have any bachelors in our Cabinet unless it's entirely necessary.

Here's a pound!
Bring back the rope! Let's go!
Your man on the door-step!

Henry Root.

Copies to: Mr Laurie McMenemy, Mr Paul Johnson and Mrs Whitehouse.

10 DOWNING STREET

10th May 1979

Dear Mr Root,

The Prime Minister has asked me to
thank you very much for your kind
letter of 4th May. Your message
of congratulations is greatly
appreciated and thank you very much
for sending us another £1 for our
Party funds.

With best wishes.

Yours Sincerely,
Richard Ryder

Richard Ryder
Political Office

Henry Root Esq

SOUTHAMPTON FOOTBALL CLUB LIMITED
Founded 1885

Registered office:
The Dell, Milton Road,
Southampton SO9 4XX

telephones:
(0703) 23408 & 28108

commercial office:
(0703) 36616

Manager:
Lawrie McMenemy

Commercial Manager:
Malcolm Price

Secretary:
Brian Truscott

LM/VG.

Dear Mr. Root.

16th May. 1979.

Thank you for your considerations and I am very flattered that you
put my name forward to Mrs. Thatcher. Should she decide to call on me
perhaps you could let me know as soon as possible before I make too many
plans for next season!

Seriously, I think she must have chosen her Cabinet by now and, like
yourself, I do hope she does a good job.

Best wishes.

Yours sincerely.

Gardner

L. McMenemy.
Manager.   (Signed in his absence.)

Directors: A.A. Woodford (Chairman), John Corbett, B.G.W. Bowyer TD, JP,
Lt. Col. Sir George Meyrick Bart. MC, F.G.L. Askham FCA, E.T.Bates.

VAT Reg. No: 188 5098 14
Reg No: 53301 England

139 Elm Park Mansions
Park Walk
London, S.W.10.

The First Sea Lord,
The Admiralty,   17th April 1979.
Whitehall,
London, S.W.1.

My Lord,
        I was alarmed to read a recent article in 'The Spectator'
by Mrs Thatcher's chiropodist, Dr Patrick Cosgrave, concerning
the imminent outbreak of hostilities with the Soviets.
        Has a definite date been fixed? Mrs Root is pressing me
to take her on a sun-shine holiday for two to the Canary Isles,
but as an ex-serving officer I naturally don't want to be out
of the country when the balloon goes up.
        I may say that in the performance of my National Service
it was my pleasure to be under the legendary Captain 'Crap'
Myers VC in the Med. He it was, as you'll remember, who during
the last show took a bolshie rating onto the casing of his sub-
marine and shot him as dead as a skunk - or so the story goes.
        I'm on red alert here and can leave for my ship at the
drop of a bollard, but I shall need to know where to go and how
to interpret my coded orders. No point in ex-serving officers
all over the country receiving a telegram from the Admiralty
reading: "Pigshit! Scuttle!' and not being able to decipher
it.
        I am awaiting your signal, my Lord.
        Let's not have a cock-up like last time!
        Yours for the defence of this once great country!

        Henry Root

        Henry Root. (Ex-Sub Lt, RNVR.)
PS. I know what Navy efficiency is like so I am enclosing a stamp
to expedite the promulgation of my orders.

NO REPLY!

139 Elm Park Mansions
Park Walk
London, S.W.10.

The Rt Hon Francis Pym,
The Ministry of Defence,
Whitehall,
London, S.W.1.

8th May 1979.

Dear Mr Pym,

May I say how much more easily in our beds we ordinary folk
will sleep now that we once again have a Minister of Defence ready
to stand up to the Soviets?

Tourist in Whitehall: "Excuse me, can you tell me which side
the War Office is on?"

Englishman: "Ours, I hope."

A joke, possibly, but not, you will agree, a very funny one.

On 17th April, having read an article in 'The Spectator' by
Mrs Thatcher's chiropodist, Dr Patrick Cosgrave, about the imminent
outbreak of hostilities with the Warsaw Pact countries, I wrote to
the First Sea Lord alerting him to my availability and requesting
information as to what would be the signal telling me to join my
ship (I am an ex-submarine officer.)

To my amazement, I received no reply! Under a Socialist
Government it was not so surprising, I suppose, that we would once
again have been up the creek, due to those in charge of our affairs
having been caught with their trousers down.

You, Sir, will change all this, I know. I would be most
grateful if you would look into this matter for me and let me know
why ordinary folk like me, prepared to fight for our country, should
be treated with such high-handed contempt by the authorities.

I look forward to hearing from you, Sir.

Stand up for our country!

Support the Iron Lady!

Yours for a good scrap,

Henry Root

Henry Root.

NAVAL PERSONNEL DIVISION 2
MINISTRY OF DEFENCE
Old Admiralty Building Spring Gardens London SW1A 2BE

Telephone (Direct Dialling) 01-218
        (Switchboard)   01-218 9000 } ext 3040

H Root Esq
139 Elm Park Mansions
Park Walk
LONDON SW10

Your reference

Our reference D/NP2/12/8/47

Date 16 May 1979

Dear Mr Root

The Secretary of State for Defence has asked me to
thank you for your encouraging letter of 8 May and I
am to inform you that your willingness to serve in
the Royal Navy in the event of hostilities has been
noted.

I can assure you that no slight was intended by the
delay in answering your earlier letter and you should
shortly receive a reply from the Office of the
First Sea Lord.

Yours faithfully

G. W. Owens

G W OWENS

From: Captain W.A. Higgins, Royal Navy

Secretary to First Sea Lord
MINISTRY OF DEFENCE
Main Building, Whitehall, London SW1A 2HB
Telephone (Direct Dialling) 01-218
(Switchboard) 01-218 9000

No. 3300/13/2

16th May 1979.

Dear Mr Root,

First Sea Lord was most grateful for your letter of
17th April offering your services should hostilities break
out and he has asked me to pass on his thanks. However,
in view of your age I am sorry to say that there is no
prospect of us being able to employ you in the Reserves
despite your earlier service.

I hope you will be relieved to learn that we have no
reason to believe that war is imminent but the only sure
way to deter any possible Soviet adventurism in the future
is by keeping our defences well up. The fact that our
Government intends to do this is surely emphasised by the
prominence given to Defence in yesterday's Queen's Speech.

Yours sincerely,

Bill Higgins.

Henry Root, Esq.

139 Elm Park Mansions
Park Walk
London, S.W.10.

8th May 1979.

Lord Hailsham,
The House of Lords,
London, S.W.1.

My Lord,
        May I say what a great pleasure it is to have once again a
man with a broad bottom on the woolsack?

        May I also say what a relief it is to ordinary folk such as
myself to have a Lord Chancellor with some determination to uphold
Law and Order?

        As the enclosed letter will show, I wrote to your Socialist
predecessor on 28th March on a matter of great public concern. It
was naive of me, perhaps, to expect a reply. While expressing a safe,
generalised concern for the common man when canvassing his vote,
Socialists, in my experience, treat him individually with the utmost
contempt, ignoring, when they come to power, his hopes, his fears,
his worries and his desires.

        I know that you, my Lord, are a public servant of a very
different kidney, and I look forward to hearing that you, unlike
your uncaring predecessor, will be taking strong action in this
disgraceful episode concerning Judge Joseph Zigmund (sic) and this
country's finest policeman, Mr James Anderton.

        Bring back the rope!

        Yours faithfully,

        Henry Root

        Henry Root.

Enc: Letter dated 28/3/79 to the Lord Chancellor.

COPY.

139 Elm Park Mansions
Park Walk
London, S.W.1.

The Lord Chancellor,
The House of Lords,
London, S.W.1.   28th March 1979.

My Lord,

        As an ordinary member of the public, I must protest in
the strongest possible terms at the unwarranted rebuke Mr James
Anderton (the Chief Constable of Manchester and this country's
finest policeman) and his devoted body of men recently received
from so-called Judge Joseph Zigmund.

        Allow me, my Lord, to remind you of the relevant details.
After much diligent police work (which involved fifty of Manchester's
best detectives lurking for an irksome nine months in a public
house, when they might have been more amusingly employed picking
prostitutes off the streets, raiding family newsagents in search
of offensive material and visiting so-called massage parlours) a
Mrs Lillian Semmonds (sic) was brought before the court, accused
of the vile offence of controlling a prostitute.

        Fining her a derisory £50, the Judge proceeded to tell the
police that they had been wasting everyone's time and then observed
that the prostitute and Mrs Semmonds had anyway been enjoying a
lesbian relationship! As though that mitigated the offence!

        As you will agree, my Lord, this evil woman should have
received a five year prison sentence for controlling a prostitute
and another five years (to run consecutively) for being a lesbian.

        Who is this Judge Joseph Zigmund? Why doesn't he practise
law in his own country? Is it a consequence of our joining the
Common Market that foreigners are now allowed to preside over our
courts?

        With the greatest respect, my Lord, I await your explanation
and to hearing what action you are taking to punish Judge Joseph
Zigmund and to defend the good name of Mr James Anderton: a man
who has been compared (by himself) to Christ and who, single-handed,
is engaged on the lonely task of combatting the forces of darkness.

        Yours faithfully,

        Henry Root

        Henry Root.

LORD CHANCELLOR'S DEPARTMENT
Neville House Page Street London SW1P 4LS

Telephone Direct line 01-211
Switchboard 01-211 3000

Your reference

Our reference

Mr H Root,
139, Elm Park Mansions,
Park Walk,
LONDON SW10.

Date   9th May 1979

Dear Mr. Root

I am writing on behalf of the Lord Chancellor to thank you for your letter of 28th March and apologise for the delay in replying.

I hope you will understand when I say from the outset that because our system of justice is based upon the independence of the courts from Government, it would be seen as a serious breach of this principle of judicial independence if the Lord Chancellor or any official of his department were to express views on the propriety of a sentence for any particular offence.

Parliament has given to all courts a complete discretion in the matter of sentencing subject in general to the maximum sentences which may be imposed for particular offences. The appropriate sentence for any individual case must be dependent on the circumstances of that case and the court, which has before it the full facts of the offence and usually the assistance of reports about the defendant's personal background and character, is in the best position to decide the correct way of dealing with him.

I do not know whether or not your attention was drawn to this case from newspaper reports, but if so, you will appreciate such reports must, of necessity, be brief and cannot possibly reflect all the conflicting factors that judges must consider when passing sentence.

It is not possible for me to be more helpful.

Yours sincerely

M A STEWART

Lord Hailsham,
The House of Lords,
London, S.W.1.

139 Elm Park Mansions
Park Walk
London, S.W.10.

10th May 1979.

Dear Lord Hailsham,
    Well done! I wrote to your predecessor on 28th March with a stiff complaint and what happened?
    Nothing!
    I then put the whole matter in your hands and what happened?
    I got a reply by return of post!
    That's the Tory way! Keep it up!
    Support Mrs Thatcher!
    Yours sincerely,

Henry Root

Henry Root.

Curtis Brown Ltd,
1 Craven Hill,
London, W.2.

139 Elm Park Mansions
Park Walk
London, S.W.10.

8th May 1979.

Dear Sir or Madam,

Please find enclosed a copy of my original stage play 'The English Way of Doing Things'.

It is a light-hearted romp in two acts about a Police Commissioner who sets forth in good shape to arrest the inmates of a bawdy-house but is flummoxed by the fact that they out-rank him socially. In a hilarious denouement he finds himself taking the bookings!

I would like to offer the part of the Police Commissioner to Sir Robert Mark.

As you will see, it's a small but telling part towards the end of the play, and I would venture to suggest exactly the sort of key but technically undemanding role that Sir Robert should be essaying at this stage of his acting career.

I think he could handle it, but we would of course require him to read for us.

I look forward to hearing from you.

Yours faithfully,

Henry Root

Henry Root.

CURTIS BROWN
LIMITED
1 Craven Hill London W2 3EP
Telephone 01-262 1011

11th May 1979

Henry Root, Esq.,
139 Elm Park Mansions,
Park Walk,
London, S.W.10.

Dear Mr. Root,

Thank you very much for sending us THE ENGLISH WAY OF DOING THINGS. I am sorry to say that Sir Robert Mark is away in Australia for the next few months and does not in any case feel that his talents lie in the direction of acting.

I am therefore returning your script and I am sorry to give you such a negative answer.

Yours sincerely,

Kate Marsh

Kate Marsh

A MEMBER OF THE CURTIS BROWN GROUP LTD LONDON SYDNEY NEW YORK

Directors Graham Watson (Chairman) Peter Grose (Managing) Diana Baring Andrew Best Felicity Bryan
Richard Odgers Michael Shaw Mollie Waters George Webster

Telex 261536 Cables Browncurt, London W2 Registered Office address as above Registered in London 1030815

139 Elm Park Mansions
Park Walk
London, S.W.10.

Head of Script Unit,
BBC Television Centre,
London, W.12.

9th May 1979.

Dear Sir,

Last night, Mrs Root and I were watching the excellent
American TV (television) show 'McMillan & Wife', when I was
struck by a sharp idea!

How about an English version of the show, called 'McNee
& Wife', based of the crime-fighting exploits of our own Commissioner? Over the past few weeks I've been in close touch with
Sir David McNee about his somewhat stodgy, not 'one 'o the People'
image and I know he's keen to come across as less of a big Glasgow
pudding to the general public. For this reason, I'm sure he'd
cooperate if you came up with some good scripts based on his
working day, showing him (like Rock Hudson) solving crimes and
bringing wrong-doers to book with the able assistance of his
lady wife and the family cook.

I happen to know he's very busy at the moment, so he might
not have time to play the central role (though I could put it to
him on my behalf.) It doesn't really matter, because I've had
a <u>second</u> sharp idea! Now that he's an actor, who better to play
the main character than Sir Robert Mark?

What do you say? I have a lot of clout with Sir Robert's
agents, Curtis Brown, and I'll get straight on to them as soon
as you give me the go-ahead.

As for the '& wife' character in the series, I doubt whether
Lady Mark (not being a thespian like her husband) could handle it.
Casting the part authentically should present no problems, however.
Mrs Root is familiar with Lady Mark from afternoon bingo sessions
in Esher and she tells me that either Hylda Baker or Thora Hird
could portray her to the life. Whichever you preferred. Let's
not butt heads over a minor character.

I look forward to receiving your go-ahead!

Yours sincerely,

Henry Root

Henry Root.

BBC TV

BRITISH BROADCASTING CORPORATION
TELEVISION CENTRE WOOD LANE LONDON W12 7RJ
TELEPHONE 01-743 8000 TELEX 265781
TELEGRAMS AND CABLES TELECASTS LONDON TELEX

Reference 35/JS/GE

28th June, 1979

Dear Mr. Root,

I have received your letter of the 1st June and seen a copy of the
letter to the Director General. As we receive 8,000 scripts a year
which we deal with in strict rotation there is inevitably some delay
in replying to authors. However, we have looked at your idea and
I have to tell you that it is not remotely possible for television
in this country for legal and copyright reasons not to mention the
fact that it is our normal practice to only employ actors who are
Equity members. Regarding copyright this is a very shady area and
there is no strict copyright in ideas. For a brief outline of
copyright law I refer you to the Writers' and Artists' Yearbook which
should be available from your local public library.

Yours sincerely,

JOHN SCOTNEY
Head of Television Script Unit

139 Elm Park Mansions
Park Walk
London, S.W.10.

The Managing Director,   3rd May 1979.
Keyser Ullman Ltd,
25 Milk Street,
London, E.C.2.

Dear Sir,
         I wish to acquire the publishing house of Jonathan Cape Ltd,
of 30 Bedford Square, London, W.C.1.
         You have been recommended to me as people who can handle a
delicate situation, so I'd be happy for you to act for me in the
matter.
         Don't charge in like a bull at a gate. Use a little stealth.
I don't want Cape to see me coming, so in the first instance just
'ask around' about the strength of the present set-up. Who the
present shareholders are, whether we can 'get anything on them' etc
etc. I don't have to teach you your business.
         We'll discuss your fees in the matter when you get in touch
with me with your initial report.
         I look forward to hearing from you.
         Yours faithfully,

         Henry Root

         Henry Root.

NO REPLY!

<u>VERY URGENT</u>.

139 Elm Park Mansions
Park Walk
London, S.W.10.

The Managing Director,
Keyser Ullman Ltd,
25 Milk Street,
London, E.C.2.

8th May 1979.

Dear Sir,

Please ignore for the moment my letter of 3rd May with reference to my takeover of Jonathan Cape Ltd.

I have only just read the Department of Trade's so-called 'Selmes Report' and in the circumstances you will quite understand that I cannot allow you to proceed on my behalf until I have had you cleared.

I will be in touch with you with further instructions once I have checked out your present standing with the Department of Trade.

<u>Do nothing until you hear from me again</u>.

Yours faithfully,

Henry Root

Henry Root.

139 Elm Park Mansions
Park Walk
London, S.W.10.

The Managing Director,
Hambros Bank Ltd,
41 Bishopsgate,
London, E.C.2.

9th May 1979.

Dear Sir,

For personal reasons which needn't concern you I am anxious
to acquire the book publishing house of Jonathan Cape Ltd.

You were not, in fact, my original choice to handle this
matter on my behalf. I first contacted the firm of Keyser
Ullman Ltd, but having read the so-called 'Selmes Report' I
decided to take my business elsewhere.

Not wishing to slip twice on the same banana skin, I had
my people run you through the computer. I have the print-out
on my desk now and I am glad to be able to tell you that you've
come up brand new. Well done! Indeed my people could find
nothing on you to suggest you're anything other than an honest
and diligent enterprise with no bad eggs under the table or
skeletons of an embarrassing nature in the cupboard.

In the circumstances I'd be happy for you to negotiate
the purchase of Jonathan Cape Ltd on my behalf. Perhaps you
could find out (without in the first instance divulging the
name of your client) the names of the present shareholders,
whether they could be 'induced' to sell, how many shares I
would have to buy to gain control and what the total cost to
myself would be.

I look forward to receiving your initial report and to
hearing what your own charges will be if we're successful.

Yours faithfully,

Henry Root

Henry Root.

Hambros Bank Limited

Your ref.

Our ref. CFD/ARB/MEB

41 Bishopsgate London EC2P 2AA
Telephone 01-588 2851 Telex 883851
Telegrams Hambro London EC2

11th May 1979

Henry Root, Esq.,
139 Elm Park Mansions,
Park Walk,
London, S.W.10.

Dear Sir,

Your letter of 9th May addressed to the Managing Director has been passed to me. Jonathan Cape is a wholly owned subsidiary of Chatto, Bodley Head & Jonathan Cape Ltd. and I would have thought it unlikely that it would be for sale on its own.

However, if you want to discuss this matter further, please do not hesitate to contact me.

Yours faithfully,

A.R. Beevor,
Director.

139 Elm Park Mansions
Park Walk
London, S.W.10.

The Department of Trade,
1 Victoria Street,
London, S.W.1.

25th May 1979.

Sir,

I seek your advice on a matter of considerable urgency.

A week or two ago - before the publication of the so-called 'Selmes Report' - I instructed the merchant banking house of Keyser Ullman Ltd to purchase Jonathan Cape Ltd, publishers of 30 Bedford Square, London, W.C.1., on my behalf.

I was naturally most concerned when I read the Selmes Report and now wonder whether I should leave the matter in the hands of Keyser Ullman.

Could you let me know (confidentially, of course) how Keyser Ullman shape up at the moment?

I cannot believe that Mr Edward du Cann - the man, let it not be forgotten, who put Mrs Thatcher where she is today - could have been associated with an enterprise that reflected incompetence.

I look forward to hearing from you.

Yours faithfully,

Henry Root

Henry Root.

DP

DEPARTMENT OF TRADE
COMPANIES DIVISION
2 - 14 Bunhill Row London EC1Y 8LL

Telephone 01-606 4071 ext 12

Henry Root Esq
139 Elm Park Mansions
Park Walk
London
SW10

Your reference

Our reference COS 452 of
1978

Date 6 June 1979

Dear Mr Root

RE: FERGUSON & GENERAL INVESTMENTS LTD
(formerly known as Dowgate & General Investments Ltd)
C S T INVESTMENTS LTD

Thank you for your letter of 25th May. I regret however, that the Department is unable to advise you as to whether or not, in the light of the Inspectors' Report, to proceed with the purchase, through Keyser UllmanLtd, of the Publishers, Jonathan Cape Ltd.

Yours sincerely

M B WOOLF

139 Elm Park Mansions
Park Walk
London, S.W.10.

The Managing Director,
Keyser Ullman Ltd,   12th June 1979.
25 Milk Street,
London, E.C.2.

Dear Sir,
          Please ignore completely my previous letters to you on the
subject of my purchase of Jonathan Cape Ltd.
          My man at the Department of Trade has now written to me as
follows:
          'I regret that the Department is unable to advise you as
to whether or not, in the light of the Inspector's Report, to
proceed with the purchase, through Keyser Ullman Ltd, of the
publishers, Jonathan Cape Ltd'.
          In the circumstances I have decided to instruct Hambros Ltd
to act in this matter for me.
          If you have already contacted (against my instructions) any
of the principles involved in the matter, I must ask you to write
to them immediately explaining that your company is in no way
associated with Henry Root Wet Fish Ltd.
          Yours faithfully,

          Henry Root

          Henry Root.

NO REPLY!

139 Elm Park Mansions
Park Walk
London, S.W.10.

Peter Barnes Esq,
The DPP's Office,   11th May 1979.
4 Queen Anne's Gate,
London, S.W.1.

Dear Mr Barnes,
        Mrs Root and I were both flabbergasted by your 'performance'
on 'TV Eye' last night.
        I find it extraordinary that at a time when our Leader, Mrs
Thatcher, has appealed to the public to support the police you, a
public person, should see fit to go on television to blackguard
them.
        No doubt your assessment, ringingly broadcast to the country
at large, that 95% of the Metropolitan CID are as bent as a kangar-
oo's hind-leg is largely correct. Do you really believe, however,
that it is conducive to law and order for the man in the street to
be aware of this? Could anything be better calculated to undermine
the thin blue line which stands between us and the abolition of
pay-beds than for the public at large to know that the Met employs
more criminals than it catches?
        I look forward to receiving an explanation, Sir, for your
extraordinary outburst.
        Support Mrs Thatcher!
        Yours sincerely,

        Henry Root

        Henry Root.

Director of Public Prosecutions
4-12 Queen Annes Gate London SW1H 9AZ

Telephones Direct line   01-213 5110 or 7363
Switchboard 01-213 3000

Henry Root Esq.
139 Elm Park Mansions
Park Walk
LONDON S.W.10

Your reference

Our reference   PAD(M)

Date   14th May 1979

Dear Mr. Root,

    I answer to your letter of 11th May, I can assure you that in the T.V. Eye programme I neither said nor implied that 95% of the Metropolitan CID are corrupt.

    Indeed my personal view is that the percentage of corrupt policemen is very small although, as I did point out in the interview, it is very hard to get sufficient evidence to ensure the conviction of those few.

    The overwhelming majority of the police do a magnificent job and they fully deserve the support and confidence of the public.

Yours sincerely,

P.R. Barnes

P.R. BARNES

139 Elm Park Mansions
Park Walk
London, S.W.10.

The Rt Hon William Whitelaw,
The Home Office,   18th May 1979.
Whitehall,
London, S.W.1.

Dear Mr Whitelaw,
        Well done! You gave me your assurance in your letter of 2nd
April that when you came to power you 'intended to build up the
strength and quality of the police to give them a better opportunity
to investigate and prevent crime'. Already you have raised their
pay! Congratulations! Soon the 'thin blue line' will become the
'thick blue line'! How splendid to have a Government which fulfils
the promises in its manifesto!

        However. In your letter to me of 27th April you wrote:

        'I can confirm that our Conservative Party will take action
against pornography'.

        Excellent. But what bothers me is this. I read recently that
60% of all drugs on the black-market had been put there by the police.
No sooner are drugs seized, it seems, than they are recycled onto
the street by the arresting officers!

        Can you assure me that the same thing won't happen with porn-
ography? It would be a scandal, in my opinion, if all the material
confiscated from family bookshops turned up a few weeks later, and,
as is the case with drugs apparently, at a grossly inflated price,
due to the Porn Squad's profit margin having to be tacked on the top.

        I know our Leader, Mrs Thatcher, is in favour of private ent-
erprise, but this is the free market gone mad! I don't want to see
the price of 'Rendezvous' going through the roof just because some
ambitious Detective Inspector (spurred on, no doubt, by Mrs Thatcher's
exhortations that he should stand on his own two feet) is buying a
new split-level maisonette with lounge-diner in Godolming.

        One would have somewhat greater faith in the average policeman's
awareness of what constitutes an acceptable profit had not Mr Peter
Barnes of the DPP's office gone on television last week to announce
in 'TV Eye' that in his opinion most of the Metropolitan CID were
as bent as corkscrews.

        Yours for the Market Economy Within Reasonable Limits!

        Henry Root

        Henry Root.

Kenneth Rose Esq,
The Sunday Telegraph,
Fleet Street,
London, E.C.4.

139 Elm Park Mansions
Park Walk
London, S.W.10.

14th May 1979.

Dear Mr Rose,

Your gossip column in 'The Sunday Telegraph' is often lively. Well done! But yesterday you had an item perplexing to the self-made man such as myself who has taken well to the paper after a poor start.

Writing of Mr Gordon Richardson, the Governor of the Bank of England (nice job!), you call him a man of 'civilised tastes'.

What are these? For my sort you must spell things out. With Mrs Thatcher pouring the sherry wine it will be even more important, if one wants to hold on in the lounge-rooms of power, to know what civilised tastes are.

Don't misunderstand me, Kenneth. I don't walk around with a straw up my nose and my trousers held at the knee with harvesting twine. I know, for instance, that one shouldn't ask one's hostess for directions to the 'toilet', listen to Shirley Bassey records or tell German jokes in the presence of the Royal Family. But Mr Richardson must know more about 'civilised tastes' than this, other-wise I'd be Governor of the Bank of England. Right?

I'd appreciate some guidelines in this area and to this end I enclose three colour snaps of myself and Mrs Root taken at the Derby last year.

I want you to come straight out and tell us whether we shape up. Don't pull your punches. If you think Mrs Root looks like an old belter, you say so. Bear in mind, however, that following a bit of luck on the 4.30 she's being escorted off the course by a constable prior to being booked on a D & D infringement. Even Mr Richardson wouldn't be at his best in such a corner, I think you'll agree.

And how about me? I might say that my suit and topper are not on hire by the hour from Covent Garden or bought with coupons. No sir. They put me back a couple of hundred quid.

Perhaps I should say that I'm 45, that I've made a fortune in wet fish and, since I've sold my business and retired, that I've got time on my hands in which to devote myself to the study of 'civilised tastes'.

Let's hear from you!
Cheers!

Henry Root

Henry Root.

As far:

SUNDAY TELEGRAPH

135 FLEET STREET LONDON EC4P 4BL TELEPHONE: 01-353 4242 TELEGRAMS: TELESUN LONDON EC4
TELEX: 22874 TELENEWS LONDON

May 15, 1979

Dear Mr. Rook,

Thank you for your letter of May 14, which I interpret a holiday to answer.

By Gordon Richardson's "civilised tastes" (in the context of his possible appointment as head of an Oxford college) I meant that he is well-read with an impressive knowledge of pictures and music.

I write a weekly column and do not run correspondence courses on etiquette : so I should regard it as very impertinent on my part to suggest how others should behave in matters of speech or recreation.

All I would say of the photographs you sent me (and which I now return) is that you seem to be having more fun than most people at the Derby. Did you back the winner?

Glad to hear you made a fortune out of film. That, I suppose, is why I can no longer afford it!

Kind good wishes,
Yours sincerely,
Kenneth Rose

139 Elm Park Mansions
Park Walk
London, S.W.10.

H.R.H. The Prince of Wales,
c/o Buckingham Palace, (please forward)
London, S.W.1.   18th May 1979.

Your Royal Highness,

        Inspired by the example of your uncle, Lord Mountbatten, I
have decided to throw my flat open to the public on Saturday 9th
June.

        I reckon to pull in the Japs and the more gullible of our
American friends. The idea is to show them how an ordinary English
couple lives.

        I'll take the mugs on a conducted tour of the premises while
Mrs Root and my two youngsters, Doreen (19) and Henry Jr (15), continue doing what any average family does at weekends: that is to
say stretching the family budget by bottling plums, lolling about
painting one's finger-nails and carrying out the weekly bullworker
maintenance. Mrs Root will be bottling plums, Doreen will be oiling
her bullworker and Henry Jr will be painting his finger-nails, but
that's young people these days.

        Would you consider performing the opening ceremony? We'd be
very honoured and it would be nice for you to meet my Doreen. If
you found yourself a little short, I'd be prepared, like your uncle
Lord Mountbatten, to sock you the pound entrance fee till you
straightened up.

        I look forward to hearing from you, Sir.

        Support Mrs Thatcher!

        Yours respectfully,

        Henry Root

        Henry Root. A naval man like yourself!

PS.   Sorry to send this care of Her Majesty, but you don't seem
to be in the phone book.

BUCKINGHAM PALACE

From: The Assistant Private Secretary to H.R.H. The Prince of Wales   4th June, 1979

Dear Mr Root,

The Prince of Wales has asked me to thank
you very much for your letter to him of 18th May
in which you asked if he would be able to visit
your flat on Saturday 9th June.

I am afraid His Royal Highness will be unable
to accept your kind invitation since he has
already made his plans for that day.

Yours Sincerely

Oliver Everett

Oliver Everett

Henry Root, Esq.

139 Elm Park Mansions
Park Walk
London, S.W.10.

H.E. The Greek Ambassador,
The Greek Embassy,   30th April 1979.
1a Holland Park,
London, W.11.

Your Excellency,

I write to you on a matter which could have serious international repercussions.

Yesterday afternoon Mrs Root was hosing down the family Rolls
under my supervision when her knees gave forth, causing her to sit
in the bucket and rick her back. A massage appeared to be the answer,
so we summoned a young lady whose advertisement in the window of our
local newsagent proclaimed 'Greek Masseuse. Full Theatrical Wardrobe'.
(Mrs Root naturally didn't want some fancy man offering to oblige
her separately.)

All was proceeding according to the book, when Arianna - for
that was the young lady's name - suddenly sat athwart Mrs Root and
suggested sapphic alternatives with the door closed.

Sir, is this the Greek way of doing things? Is this some
indigenous custom of your once great country, instigated by such
celebrated homosexualists as Plato the Great and General Alexander
and kept alive by such as the big warbling pudding who crops up from
time to time on 'Top of the Pops'?

Mrs Root screeched like a gibbon and Arianna high-tailed it
out of the flat with her bag of tricks, but Mrs Root was so shaken
by the incident that I had to get my own dinner. In the circumstances
we have thought it best to cancel a sunshine holiday for two we had
planned to take this summer in your part of the world, where no doubt
swimming without clothes and the eating of raw fish is now encouraged.

I would suggest, Mr Ambassador, that you take immediate action
to dissuade those of Miss Arianna's stripe from bringing the rest of
you into disrepute.

Such incidents as the one I have described could never have
happened under the Colonels.

Yours respectfully,

Henry Root

Henry Root.

Copy to The Foreign Office.

                              139 Elm Park Mansions
                              Park Walk
                              London, S.W.10.

The Greek Ambassador,
1a Holland Park,
London, W.11.   1st June 1979.

Your Excellency,
        I am astonished that you haven't had the common civility to
reply to my letter of 30th April re Mrs Root's experience at the
hands of one of your masseuses.
        What's going on over there in Holland Park? Get a grip on
yourself, my good man!
        I look forward to hearing from you by return.
        Yours sincerely,

        Henry Root

        Henry Root.
Copy to Sir Ian Gilmour, The Foreign Office.

CONSULATE GENERAL OF GREECE

1A HOLLAND PARK, LONDON W11 3TP   TEL.: 01-727 8040

7th June, 1979

Henry Root, Esq.,
139 Elm Park Mansions,
Park Walk,
LONDON S.W.10.

Dear Sir,

We acknowledge receipt of your letters dated 30th April and 1st June addressed to His Excellency the Ambassador and which have been forwarded to me.

I am sorry for the trouble which has been caused to your wife but, as you will understand, it is not a matter of the competence of this Consulate General and I suggest that if you wish to pursue the matter you should contact the competent British authorities.

Yours faithfully,
For Consul General

P. Vlassopoulos
Consul

Foreign and Commonwealth Office
London SW1A 2AH

Telephone 01- 233-5097

Henry Root Esq
139 Elm Park Mansions
Park Walk
LONDON SW10

Your reference

Our reference

Date 6 June 1979

Dear Mr Root

I have been asked to thank you for your
letter of 1 June to Sir Ian Gilmour, the
contents of which have been noted. The
incident you describe is indeed regrettable.
I hope that Mrs Root's back is better.

Yours Sincerely

A L S Coltman
Southern European Department

139 Elm Park Mansions
Park Walk
London, S.W.10.

Mr A.L.S. Coltman,
Southern European Department,
The Foreign and Commonwealth Office,   21st June 1979.
London, S.W.1.

Dear Mr Coltman,
        Thank you for your letter of 6th June re the incident of
Mrs Root and the Greek 'masseuse'.
        She's on the mend now, you'll be relieved to hear, though
she still gets the jitters from time to time, being unable to watch
without qualms Miss Esther Rantzen on TV or confront a portion of
moussaka.
        Please thank Sir Ian Gilmour for taking an interest in this
matter. Don't bother Lord Carrington with it. I'm sure he's got
enough to worry about what with one thing and another here and there.
        Perhaps I could seek your advice on another matter while I
have your attention. Having cancelled our annual holiday for two
in Greece consequent upon Mrs Root's 'experience', we are now wondering whether the sunshine island of Ibiza might make a viable altern-
ative. Once was when the holder of a British passport could move
through Europe and other parts knowing that his person and the persons
of his family were adequately protected by the signature of Her Majesty's Foreign Secretary on page 1. Not anymore, it seems. I have
heard rumours that even in Spain matters are not, since the sad death
of General Franco, all that they might be re law and order. As so
often happens, democracy, it seems, has brought in its wake swarms
of local Pedros who roam the streets putting their hands up ladies'
skirts and infiltrating to their own ends the wallet-pockets of
package tourists.
        Can you, Sir, as a Southern European expert, tell me whether
these practices have now reached the Balearics or whether in fact
Mrs Root and I could safely visit Ibiza this summer without incident?
        Yours sincerely,

        Henry Root

        Henry Root.

Foreign and Commonwealth Office
London SW1A 2AH

Telephone 01-

Henry Root Esq
139 Elm Park Mansions
Park Walk
London SW10

Your reference

Our reference

Date

27 June 1979

Dear Mr Root

Thank you for your letter of 21 June. I am glad that Mrs Root is better.

I know no reason why you should not visit Ibiza. But the activities to which you refer are indeed apt to occur in most popular tourist centres. A travel agent should be able to advise on this aspect.

Yours Sincerely

A L S Coltman
Southern European Department

139 Elm Park Mansions
Park Walk
London, S.W.10.

C. James Anderton Q.P.M., F.B.I.M.,
Chief Constable's Office,
Chester House,
Boyer Street,
Manchester MI6 ORE.

21st May 1979.

Dear Chief Constable,

May I congratulate you on your fine showing on the TV programme 'Jaywalking' yesterday evening?

You came over as forceful and sincere - in marked contrast,
I may say, to our own Sir David McNee, who recently made a very
poor fist of being interviewed on 'Thames at 6'. He shaped up
well physically, but under Andrew Gardner's relentless probing
his brain fell out and he admitted, among other things, that half
his force was corrupt! Not very good for the morale of those
under him! You'd never fall into such an obvious trap!

One slight criticism. Questioning you about your sensible
decision to give full police protection (at a cost of hundreds of
thousands of pounds to the rate-payers) to a recent National
Front rally on your patch (as you so rightly understand, freedom
of speech - however obnoxious - <u>must</u> be protected by the law,
though this freedom must <u>never</u> be extended to pornographers), Miss
Jay said:

"Was that a moral decision or a police decision?"

My eldest, Doreen, who is reading philosophy and sociology
at Essex University, said that either this was a category mistake
(whatever that might be!) or Miss Jay was implying that a police
decision can never be a moral decision.

If my Doreen is correct (and it wouldn't be the first time,
I might add), may I ask you why you didn't thrust Miss Jay's
question back down her throat by saying something along the lines
of:

"Are you suggesting, madam, that there must always be a clear
distinction between a moral decision and a police decision? I
recognise no such distinction."

Apart from this one slight lapse - a really splendid performance! Well done!

Keep it up!

Christians demand the return of the rope!
Your pal in the soft south!

Henry Root

Henry Root.

C James Anderton Q.P.M., F.B.I.M.
Chief Constable

Chief Constable's Office
P O Box 22 (S.West PDO)
Chester House
Boyer Street
Manchester M16 0RE
Telephone 061-872 5050

22nd May 1979.

Dear Mr. Root,

It was kind of you to write to me on 21st May and I appreciate your good wishes.

Your daughter Doreen is absolutely right in her opinion of my handling of the question to which you specifically refer. The trouble is that,in a lengthy television interview during which questions come thick and fast, it is not possible always to sort out one's thoughts quickly enough to meet the situation correctly. In any event, the whole thing was pre-recorded and later chopped about in such a way that one cannot guarantee that the questions and answers are put together properly. You will know television interviewers often film their own questions again later to complete the programme.

If I had dealt with the question better to meet the point raised by your daughter, I am quite sure it would not have featured in the programme at all.

Thank you for your interest.

Yours sincerely,

Chief Constable.

Henry Root, Esq.,
139 Elm Park Mansions,
Park Walk,
London. S.W.10.

139 Elm Park Mansions
Park Walk
London, S.W.10.

The Producer,
'Brass Tacks',   23rd May 1979.
BBC,
Manchester.

Dear Sir,
        I wish to protest most strongly at the scandalous treatment
this country's finest policeman, Mr James Anderton, received on
your programme last night.
        To sit a fine Christian gentleman down in close proximity to
an unsavoury crowd of prostitutes was bad enough. Even worse was
to allow him to be humilaited intellectually by the afore-mentioned
rabble (when you must have known perfectly well that it is not given
to mere policemen, as it is to street-walkers, to think coherently
on their feet.) Worst of all was your irresponsible decision not
to cut out the ringingly audible aside made by one of the ladies
of the night, who suddenly turned to the painted strumpet sitting
on her left and said, in a whisper which must have echoed round the
country:
        "This sanctimonious, dirty-minded half-wit really gets on
my tits! I hate to think how <u>he</u> gets his rocks off!"
        Your programme, apart from being an aid and comfort to every
prostitute in the land, Sir, must have put the cause of Law and Order
back by fifty years.
        I await your explanation.
        Yours disgusted,

        Henry Root

        Henry Root.
P.S. I would be grateful if you could supply me with the phone
number of the young lady with red hair who sat in the centre and
did most of the talking. I would like to contact her with reference
to my own researches.

20th June, 1979.

Mr. Henry Root,
139, Elm Park Mansions,
Park Walk,
London, S.W.10.

Dear Mr. Root,

In the absence of our Editor, Roger Laughton, your letter has been passed to me by the Programme Controller's office for reply.

As you know, at the end of BRASS TACKS we advertise a service to viewers who wish to express a point of view on the subject under discussion. That's in a programme called RETURN CALL transmitted on the Monday following the programme. In fact, an excerpt from your letter was used in that programme on 28th May 1979.

> "Your programme, apart from being an aid and comfort to every prostitute in the land, Sir, must have put the cause of Law and Order back fifty years."

As you will realise the response to such a subject was overwhelming and we received several hundred letters, which makes it quite impossible to furnish individual replies to all of them. May I say that of all the people who have written with a point of view on the subjects we have covered, this is the first time that anyone has objected to not getting a personal reply.

To take up some of the other points in your first letter, a copy of which we retain on our files, I have reviewed the tape of the original transmission and can at no point hear anyone saying:

> "This sanctimonious, dirty-minded half-wit really gets on my tits! I hate to think how <u>he</u> gets his rocks off!"

Finally, I am afraid it is not our policy to release the telephone numbers of programme guests. However, if you wish, I am quite happy to forward a letter from you to the young lady in question and then leave it to her discretion as to whether or not she chooses to reply.

Yours sincerely,

Eric Robson,
Presenter,
BRASS TACKS.

139 Elm Park Mansions
Park Walk
London, S.W.10.

Mr Eldon Griffiths MP,
The House of Commons,
London, S.W.1.

26th May 1979.

Dear Eldon,

I was delighted to read in the paper this week that you are
already planning to raise the 'restoration of hanging' issue in
the House. Well done! Once again ordinary folk have a Government
which cares a little for their safety.

I have a suggestion to make, on which I'd appreciate your
comments. One of the arguments for capital punishment rests on
the deterrent value of the rope. Couldn't it be argued that hanging is too swift a method of execution to deter the really hard-
line criminal?

I expect you were as impressed as I was to read of the recent
execution in Florida of a character called John Spenkelink in the
electric chair. It seems a full six minutes passed before Spenkelink was dead, during which time he hopped about like a prawn on
a hot-plate.

That will have taught him to think twice in future before
shooting innocent people.

Wouldn't the prospect of being slowly fried to a crisp be
more alarming to the terrorists and sex fiends who are making it
impossible for decent folk to walk our streets than the mere
prospect of dangling at the end of a rope?

Let me have your views on this.

Support Mrs Thatcher!

Yours for the introduction of the chair!

Henry Root

Henry Root.

Eldon Griffiths M.P.

acknowledges with thanks the receipt of your communication

of the 26th May

the contents of which have been noted.

8/77 12m 335617 LP1-2029

H.C. 85

139 Elm Park Mansions
Park Walk
London, S.W.10.

Mr George Hardy,
Derby County Football Club,
The Baseball Ground,   28th May 1979.
Derby.

Dear George,
        I'm a busy man, but you're in a deep hole with the Rams and
I'm prepared to dig you out. I'm hereby nominating myself for the
job of manager, as advertised.
        Right. Down to cases. You'll want to know what experience
I've had of running a football club.
        None at all!
        So what? The name of the game is motivation and psychology,
and that I know about. Why do you suppose Mr Clough consistently
delivers the goods? Because he terrorises the lads into turning
it on for him, that's why. I'll be the same. I'll have the lads
so psyched up they'll run round the park like demented threshing-
machines, reducing even Liverpool's Red Army to a bunch of dancing
woofters.
        In one respect only will I carry on with the policies of my
predecessor, the Doc. I'll get rid of all the good players. (He
only left two behind - Daly and the boy Hill - so this won't take
long.) Psychology again, you see. The players who stay behind
will feel less bad about their uselessness out there on the park.
        I gather you've got a few bad eggs under the board-room table.
They'll have to go. Leave this to me.
        It so happens that I'll be in Derby on business on Tuesday
12th June. If I don't hear from you to the contrary, I'll assume
it will be okay for me to drop in and see you at the Baseball
Ground at about 12.30. We can finalise the details - salary, perks,
kick-backs etc - then.
        Let me know if you can't make it. I'd be as sick as a parrot
to run into your office only to discover that you were visiting
your 'masseuse'.
        Up the Rams!
        It's all about winning!
        Yours,

        Henry Root

        Henry Root.

DERBY COUNTY FOOTBALL CLUB LIMITED

All Communications to be addressed to the Secretary

Registered in England No. 49139

Our ref: GH/SAB

12th July 1979

Dear Sir

We thank you for your letter applying for the position of Manager with our Club.

We regret to inform you that your application was unsuccessful, the Club having appointed Mr. Colin Addison to the position.

May we thank you for your interest and we wish you every success in the future

Yours faithfully

George Hardy
Chairman

139 Elm Park Mansions
Park Walk
London, S.W.10.

Nicholas Scott MP,
The House of Commons,
London, S.W.1.

28th May 1979.

Dear Mr Scott,

During the recent election campaign you were good enough to
answer my questions most promptly.

In the event, I'm afraid I was unable to vote for you (as you
will remember, we were unable to resolve our differences over the
selective hanging issue) but you are, for better or worse, my MP,
so I wonder if I might trouble you again.

Following the adverse publicity given to the behaviour of
the Scottish football fans on Saturday last, the false and mis-
leading comparisons between the dangers of alcohol and so-called
cannabis are once again being made. The 'legalise cannabis' lobby
in the media has been quick to draw our attention to the violence,
blood-shed and damage to property caused by the high-spirited
Tartan Army, and equally quick to point out that far from inducing
this kind of anti-social behaviour cannabis, in fact, has a strangely peaceable and law-abiding effect on those who take it.

So what? A drop of the hard stuff never hurt anyone. Most
parents, as I'm sure you will agree, would infinitely prefer that
their youngsters were exposed to a bit of boisterous horse-play by
a few thousand bottle-throwing football fans than that they should
'drop out' of reality by taking cannabis.

Can I have your assurance that you will never vote for any
bill designed to legalise cannabis or one to restrict the easy
distribution of alcohol?

Support Mrs Thatcher!
Yours for a wee drop!

Henry Root

Henry Root.

House of Commons
London SW1

Nicholas Scott, MBE, MP

7 June 1979

Dear Mr Root

Thank you for your letter.

'Never' is an extravagant word in the
political lexicon, but I do fully share
your views about the dangers of legalising
cannabis and I have little fear that I shall
become hooked on the evidence of counter-
vailing opinion.

As for alochol, I must admit it would
be against my natural inclinations and
better judgement to seek to control its
consumption.

Yours sin

Nicholas Scott

Henry Root Esq.

139 Elm Park Mansions
Park Walk
London, S.W.10.

Mr 'Larry' Lamb,   25th May 1979.
The Sun,
30 Bouverie Street,
London, E.C.4.

Dear Mr Lamb,
        I wish to protest most strongly about a story which
appears on the front page of 'The Sun' today.
        Under a picture of a foreign 'actress' (no doubt French)
called Suzanne Danielle, we are informed that she lives with a
Mr Patrick Mower in a Buckinghamshire cottage.
        I don't want to know that! Nor, I may say, does Mrs Root.
        Is it due to some sub-clause in the Treaty of Rome that
we now have to be brought up to date over our breakfast corn-
flakes with the immoral arrangements of foreign 'actresses' living in this country? Such information should be tucked away
on page 3, if anywhere.
        Why can't you publish on your front page a picture of
the gracious and talented English actress, Miss Nanette Newman,
with the information that she is living with her husband, the
equally talented Mr Bryan Forbes, in a villa in Virginia Water?
        I look forward to receiving your explanation, Sir, for
this thinly veiled attack on family values.
        Support Mrs Thatcher!
        Yours sincerely,

        Henry Root

        Henry Root.
Copy to Sir David Nicholson (56, married, 3 grown-up children - Euro
candidate.)

Sir David Nicholson,
10 Fordie House,
Sloane Street,
London, S.W.1.

139 Elm Park Mansions
Park Walk
London, S.W.10.

25th May 1979.

Dear Sir David,

I enclose a copy of a letter I have today written to
Mr 'Larry' Lamb of Sun Newspapers Ltd.

Before I cast my vote for you in the coming European
election, could you let me know where you stand on this sort
of issue?

In my view the Common Market should be about morality
as well as butter mountains. What do you think?

I see from your leaflet that you speak fluent French
and have a knowledge of Germans. Do you know something we
don't know?

Support Mrs Thatcher!

Yours sincerely,

Henry Root

Henry Root. Anti-Marketeer.

NEWS GROUP NEWSPAPERS LTD
A Subsidiary of News International Ltd

Registered Office:

30 Bouverie Street, Fleet Street, London, EC4Y 8DE.

Registered No. 679215 England
Telex Sunnews 267827
Telephone 01-353 3030
EDITOR'S OFFICE

May 30th, 1979.

AL/MD

Henry Root, Esq.,
139, Elm Park Mansions,
Park Walk,
London, SW10.

Dear Mr Root

Thank you for your letter.

I understand - without necessarily accepting - your point of view.

We are in the business of supplying information. Doctor Who is a very popular programme. Mr. Mower is a very popular actor.

To record the fact of his domestic arrangement with Ms. Danielle surely does not imply approval of the arrangement.

My apologies to Mrs. Root!

With best wishes,

Yours sincerely,

Larry Lamb,
EDITOR.

DAVID
NICOLSON
LONDON CENTRAL
EURO-CONSTITUENCY

CONSERVATIVE CANDIDATE

CENTRAL COMMITTEE ROOM: 90, EBURY ST. SWIW 9QD ★ TEL: 730 8181 ★ ELECTION AGENT: B. VILLETTE

Henry Root. Esq.,
139, Elm Park Mansions,
Park Walk,
<u>LONDON S.W.10.</u>

30th May, 1979.

Dear Mr Root,

Many thanks for your letter of May 25th, and I can
only say that I too deplore the kind of article to which you refer
and which appears so often in the popular press.

I believe if we had a proper national objective once
again and concentrated on other things, we could certainly improve
standards of morality.

Yours sincerely,

David Nicolson

Published by: B. Villette, 90 Ebury Street, S.W.1. & Printed by: Errington & Martin, 25 Elsdale St., E.9.

139 Elm Park Mansions
Park Walk
London, S.W.10.

30th May 1979.

The Chairman,
The Parole Board,
50 Queen Anne's Gate,
London, S.W.1.

Dear Sir,

May I, a mere member of the general public, congratulate you
on your enlightened decision to release ex-Commander Kenneth
Drury, late of the Flying Squad?

In my opinion a policeman should never be sent to prison,
no matter what he's done. It's outrageous that he should be
obliged to mingle with common criminals, many of whom he will
have been obliged to 'fit up' in the execution of his duty.

Perhaps I could take this opportunity of suggesting parole
for the so-called Luton Post Office killers. Not because they
happen to be innocent. In the interests of law and order that's
neither here nor there. No, I suggest clemency merely on the
grounds that their sentence seemed a little harsh. Ten years
is about right for something you didn't do; twenty is definitely
too long.

I look forward to hearing your views on this suggestion.

Yours faithfully,

Henry Root

Henry Root.

Copy to Mr Timothy Raison MP.

PAROLE BOARD

Queen Anne's Gate
LONDON, SW1H 9AT

LM

Direct Line 01-213
Switchboard 01-213 3000

Your Ref ....

Any communication on the subject of this letter
should be addressed to:
THE SECRETARY

and the following reference quoted:

....

17 July 1979

Mr H Root
139 Elm Park Mansions
Park Walk
LONDON
SW10

Dear Mr Root

Thank you for your letter of 30 May to which the Chairman of the Parole Board has
asked me to reply on his behalf. The delay in replying is regretted.

I should perhaps explain that the Parole Board is an independent non-judicial advisory
body only and can only consider and recommend on cases which have been referred to it
by the Home Secretary. This applies equally to prisoners with determinate sentences
or with life sentences, and until the Home Secretary sees fit to refer the cases you
mention to it, the Parole Board has no authority to comment on the matter of their
parole suitability.

I should also add that the question of a prisoner's guilt or innocence is not a
matter for the Parole Board. The Board can only proceed on the premise that parole
candidates are guilty of the crimes they have been convicted of by the Courts and
sentenced accordingly.

I have copied this correspondence to the Home Office for their information.

Yours sincerely

Marcella Hargreaves

HOME OFFICE
Queen Anne's Gate London SW1H 9AT

Direct line 01-213
Switchboard 01-213 3000

H Root Esq
139 Elm Park Mansions
Park Walk
LONDON
SW10

Your reference

Our reference
PDP/M 0910/9/14
Date

27 July 1979

Dear Sir

You wrote to Mr Raison on 1 June asking for his comments on a copy of a letter which you had sent to the Chairman of the Parole Board.

On the first point (that police officers convicted of offences should not be sent to prison) the sentence to be imposed in a particular case is, within the limits provided by the law and subject to the right of appeal, for the Court to decide in the light of all the information before it about the offence and the offender. It would be wholly inappropriate for the Home Secretary, or any Government Minister for that matter, to attempt to interfere with the Court's discretion in an individual case.

On the second point (that those convicted of the murder of the Luton sub-postmaster should now be released on parole) prisoners serving life sentences are not eligible for parole as such but are released on a life licence under the terms of which they may be recalled to prison at any time during the remainder of their lives should their conduct make this necessary. But the Home Secretary cannot order the release of a life sentence prisoner unless he is recommended to do so by the Parole Board and after he has consulted the Lord Chief Justice and, if he is available, the trial judge. Each case is dealt with individully on its own merits and, in considering the case of any life sentence prisoner, the Parole Board and the Home Secretary must proceed on the basis that the prisoner was rightly convicted. The cases of those convicted of the murder of the Luton sub-postmaster will be considered in precisely the same way as those of all other prisoners serving life sentences for murder.

Yours faithfully

V.K Storey

MRS V K STOREY

Root House
139 Elm Park Mansions
Park Walk
London, S.W.10.

Lord Grade,
ACC Ltd,
ATV House,
London, W.1.   1st June 1979.

Dear Lord Grade,

I'm presently getting together a consortium of plausible businessmen to take over the publishing house of Jonathan Cape.

I don't know whether you're familiar with this company. It once enjoyed a solid reputation in the world of letters, but recently, due to lack of editorial know-how and ability to pick winning manuscripts with lucrative subsidary rights situations attached, it has gone back badly.

It is my opinion, however, that with the right go-go management (me) directing its affairs, in place of the grey-beards and dizzy young girls now in control, it could once again have a relevant contribution to make to the literary scene.

Would you be interested in joining the consortium? My bankers, Hambros, are pressing me for a meeting, but first I want to arrange some financial back-up. Under-capitalised, I'd be running through Hambros' door in nothing but my bowler hat and that would create a doubtful impression.

You appeal to me as a man who can make up his mind quickly (well done!) so if the concept strikes you as valid perhaps you'd like to have lunch (on me!) at the Mirabelle at 1 o'clock on Friday 15th June.

May I say how much I'm looking forward to your Euro-Gala from the Theatre Royal, Drury Lane this Sunday? Miss Petunia Clark is a splendid artiste and melodies to catch the ear always appeal to the family.

You're a true European!

I look forward to hearing from you.

Yours for family entertainment!

Henry Root

Henry Root.

ATV House
17 Great Cumberland Place
London W1A 1AG
telephone 01-262 8040
cables and telegrams
Ayteevee London W1
telex 23762

From the office of the Deputy Chairman
and Deputy Chief Executive

6th June, 1979

JFG/MANL

H. Root, Esq.,
139 Elm Park Mansions,
Park Walk,
London S.W.10

Dear Mr. Root,

Lord Grade has passed to me your letter
of the 1st June concerning your proposition
to buy the book publishing house of
Jonathan Cape Limited. We actually looked
at this particular company some twelve months
ago and decided not to attempt to purchase it.

We hope that you will be successful
in obtaining someone else to join your
consortium.

Yours sincerely,

Jack Gill.

139 Elm Park Mansions
Park Walk
London, S.W.10.

Miss Debra Byron,
Editorial,
Jonathan Cape Ltd,
30 Bedford Square,
London, W.C.1.

2nd June 1979.

Dear Miss Byron,

Thank you for your letter of 20th April with regard to my original novel, 'Day of Reckoning'. I must apologise for not getting back to you before now.

You'll be delighted to know that your prompt and courteous rejection of the book as it then stood in no way drove me from my typewriter! Rather the reverse! This, I suspect, was your intention. As you quickly perceived, you weren't dealing with silly young girl with her head filled with maudlin literary dreams of an Irish slant, but with a plain-speaking man with whom you needn't pull your editorial punches.

I know one can't expect instant success. After all, isn't it the case that Freddy Forsyth's 'The Day of the Jackass' was turned down with ill-concealed contempt by no less than 37 of the top houses including your own (well done!)

So did I give up? No sir! I had a long hard look at the piece (particularly the ending - so often the weakest part of a first book) and came to the conclusion that there might be something valid in what you said.

So I went to work! Here, after six hard weeks are the fruits of your editorial know-how and my perseverence. What I have done, as you will quickly see, is tighten up the prose and cut ruthlessly (without, I hope, destroying the book's artistic integrity) so we are left with nothing but the hard muscle of the narrative line. Now the reader is led unerringly by the nose to the book's psychological centre - our hero's actual moment of reckoning, the moment when he discovers who he really is.

Other deft touches have been to alter the main character's name to Harry Toro (this renders the work less distractingly autobiographical) and to change the name of a subsiduary character from Lorraine Pumptit (weak) to Desiree Thunderbottom (much stronger).

Okay, the ball's back in your court! Let's go!

Yours sincerely,

Henry Root

Henry Root.

Teleph

<u>DAY OF RECKONING</u>
By
<u>HENRY ROOT.</u>

<u>2nd Draft.</u>

Amazingly attractive, 45-year-old Harry Toro, chairman of Harry Toro
Wet Fish Ltd woke up in the bedroom of his luxury mansion in Maidenhead.

He began to count his blessings. His Rolls, his swimming-
pool, the expense account trips to Paris and New York with his latest
'companion', the long-legged, full-bosomed 'starlet', Desiree Thunderbottom.

Suddenly he felt guilty. He thought of the back-streets of
Barnsley in which he'd been born and in which his aged parents still
lived. Were he to get up now, take the Rolls from the garage and
drive himself, literally and metaphorically, back to his origins
would he still have anything to say to his old mum and dad, to his
mates at the local factory and to little Janet Gibbens with whom
he'd had his first 'experience' at the local Odeon?

"Who cares?" he thought, and he went happily back to sleep.

<u>THE END.</u>

Henry Root
139 Elm Park Mansions
Park Walk
London, S.W.7.

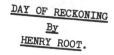

JONATHAN CAPE LIMITED
THIRTY BEDFORD SQUARE
LONDON W.C.1

Telegrams
CAPAJON, LONDON WC1B 3EL

6th June, 1979

r Henry Root,
139 Elm Park Mansions,
Park Walk, S.W.10.
London. S.W.10.

Dear Mr Root,

Thank you for your letter of 2nd June and a copy of your synopsis
for DAY OF RECKONING. We regret that we still do not think it
would be worth your while submitting your novel to us and we wish
you success in placing it with another publisher.

Yours sincerely,

Debra Byron.

Debra Byron,
Editorial.

Encl; Synopsis

Tom Maschler Graham C. Greene Liz Calder W. Robert Carr Anthony Colwell John Robinson Norman Askew
Registered in England under no. 195767 Registered office as above

139 Elm Park Mansions
Park Walk
London, S.W.10.

Petal Model Agency Ltd,
28 Walpole Street,
London, S.W.3.

6th June 1979.
(D-Day plus 35 years!)

Dear Sir or Madame,

In case you are unfamiliar with my work, let me say at
once that I am a photographer not without experience and flair,
known for the standard of my finish here and there. Also fully
equipped with Hasselblad and strobe.

You have been given to me as the people to supply the best
type of girl for outdoor photography without clothes.

Here's the concept. Now that we have joined the Common
Market it is particularly deplorable, in my opinion, that maga-
zines of the sort that male readers participate in privately with
the door shut still consider exotic locations abroad as the
proper setting for figure shooting on the sands.

What's wrong with this country? Why does it always have
to be Denise, Stephanie, Fifi and Kerry-Jane soaking up the sun
on the beaches of Ibiza and then joining the photographer, Heinz,
in the champagne a go-go bar of the Hotel Player Real?

Why not Denise, Stephanie, Fifi and Kerry-Jane in the car-
park of the Red Bull Hotel Staines and, later, enjoying a shandy
with the photographer, Henry de Root, in the Executives Bar of the
same hotel?

I invisage a lay-out for 'Penthouse' entitled 'Away Day in
Staines' and to this end I would like to book four of your best
types while the weather holds.

Please let me know what would be the price of each girl for
participating in erotic tableaux in Staines throughout the day and
early evening (nothing distasteful).

I look forward to hearing from you.

Yours sincerely,

Henry de Root

Henry de Root. Photographer.

Petal Model Agency,
28 Walpole Street,
London, S.W.3.

139 Elm Park Mansions
Park Walk
London, S.W.10.

16th June 1979.

Dear Sir or Madame,

Why haven't I heard from you in reply to my letter of
6th June with regard to the proposed lay-out in 'Penthouse'?

Never mind! I can come to you! I'll hop into your office
at 3.30 pm on Tuesday 26th June to run my eye up and down a
line-up of your best types.

Do you happen to represent the delightful lass currently
participating in the 'Lilt' commercial on TV (television)? If
you do, get her there on the 26th. She'd be fine for what I
have in mind. Also those two blonde girls - don't know their
names, I'm afraid - who apart from modelling without benefit of
clothes also form a popular singing duo. I think one of them
may be called Nina. Have them there on Tuesday week if you represent them.
one. Or if it's not her, then it's the other
Plus any others you deem appropriate to my concept.

I look forward to becoming acquainted with you and the
girls on the 26th. Kindly let me know well in advance if for
any reason this date is not suitable for you. I'd hate to run
through your door and find no one there but a couple of dozey
typists painting their finger-nails and considering their personal involvements.

Let's make money here!

Yours sincerely,

Henry de Root

Henry de Root.

PETAL

PETAL MODEL AGENCY LTD. 28 WALPOLE STREET, CHELSEA, LONDON, SW3 4QS

U.K. Bookings: Press, Television, Film, 01-730 7284 International Bookings 01-730 7285 Telex: Petal 21879
Accounts: Invoices 01-730 1902 Bought ledgers 0295 4491

Mr. Henry de Root,
139 Elm Park Mansions,
Park Walk, London, S.W.10.

18th June, 1979.

Dear Mr. de Root,

Thank you for your letter of the 16th June.

Unfortunately we do not have any models suitable for your
proposed lay-out for 'Penthouse'.

The model in the 'Lilt' advertisement is Stefanie Marrian, who
is with Askew's model agency. Also the two blond models you mentioned
are currently making a record but can be found at Bobton's.

I'm sorry we can't help you, but perhaps you could ring Geoff
Wootton Agency 736 0191.

Yours sincerely,

Dawn Wylie-Harris

Dawn Wylie-Harris

The Director of Public Prosecutions,
The DPP's Office,
4 Queen Anne's Gate,
London, S.W.1.

139 Elm Park Mansions
Park Walk
London, S.W.10.

Sir,

19th June 1979.

I have before me the so-called girlie magazine Penthouse, Vol 14 No 4, and refer specifically to 'Emma Jane's Diary' which purports to be a regular column written by a self-alleged call-girl entitled Miss Emma Jane Crampton.

I make no comment on the fact that a call-girl is allowed to advertise her services by writing a column in a widely read magazine. That the authorities allow such a state of affairs to continue hardly surprises one these days.

However, I do object most strongly to her opening remarks, which read as follows:

'Disgusted to find in my 'Observer' today a long and syco-phantic interview with the increasingly absurd Mrs Thatcher, in the course of which she keeps referring to something she calls 'ordinary folk'. It so happens that I shall shortly be interviewing Mrs Thatcher myself on behalf of 'Penthouse' and I can say here and now that if she dares to call me 'an ordinary folk' I shall lean forward and, with one deft movement, pull her knickers down.'

Can one say this? Surely any unauthorised reference to Mrs Thatcher's knickers is illegal and a threat to pull them down by a private citizen unacquainted with Mrs Thatcher tantamount to civil disorder? So-called Miss Crampton continues:

'In my experience most suburban ladies find it a most discon-certing tactic and I urge 'ordinary folk' throughout the land to adopt this highly effective form of political comment should they have the misfortune to meet Mrs Thatcher in the course of one of her vote-losing walk-abouts'.

There we have it! A direct instruction to ordinary folk everywhere (and what's wrong with being an ordinary folk, I might ask?) to pull our Leader's knickers down! And what could be more offensive than Miss Crampton's suggestion that only suburban ladies would find such treatment discouraging? She continues:

'I assure you that the manoeuvre is easier than you might suppose - the element of surpise usually proving decisive. I did it to Mrs Whitehouse outside the Old Bailey after the Gay News trial and, as you will have seen for yourselves, she hasn't been the same since'.

I look forward to receiving your assurance, Sir, that you have already started proceedings against Miss Emma Jane Crampton and the magazine for which she writes. Failing this, I must tell you that I shall have no hesitation in instigating a private prosecution.

I am not without means and am aquainted with Sir James Goldsmith.

Yours faithfully,

Henry Root.

Henry Root.

Copy to Mrs Mary Whitehouse.

NATIONAL VIEWERS' AND LISTENERS' ASSOCIATION

Hon. Treasurer
Mr R. C. Standring
'Still Waters'
Pine Walk, East Horsley
LEATHERHEAD, Surrey
Tel. East Horsley 2573

President:

Vice-President: Miss C. J. FitzGerald

Hon. Gen. Sec.
Mrs Mary Whitehouse
Ardleigh, COLCHESTER
Essex, CO7 7RH
Tel. Colchester 230 123

26th June 1979

Mr. Henry Root,
139 Elm Park Mansions,
Park Walk,
London SW10.

Dear Mr. Root,

Thank you very much for your letter of 19th June and
for the copy of the letter you have sent to the Director of
Public Prosecutions.

Miss Crampton's story is pure fabrication as far as I
am concerned - I am grateful for your concern over this but I
am of the opinion that any legal action on our part over this
would simply give publicity to this very stupid woman.

Yours sincerely,

Mary Whitehouse

The Director of Public Prosecutions
acknowledges receipt of Mr. HENRY ROOT 's
communication of 19th JUNE 1979

4/12 QUEEN ANNES GATE,
LONDON SW1H 9AZ

2 6 JUN 1979

(2437) 3-31866Z/000826 1/74 2m NC5 821

139 Elm Park Mansions
Park Walk
London, S.W.10.

The Director of Public Prosecutions,
The DPP's Office,
4 Queen Anne's Gate,
London, S.W.1.   7th August 1979.

Dear Sir,

I wrote to you on 19th June 1979 in the matter of so-called
Miss Emma Jane Crampton's suggestion in the 'girlie' magazine
'Penthouse' that ordinary folk should, if presented with the
opportunity, pull Mrs Thatcher's knickers down (surely there's
a 'D' Notice on these?)

I said that unless I had your immediate assurance that you
were about to institute proceedings against Miss Crampton and
the magazine for which she writes, I would commence a private
prosecution myself.

On 27th June I received a curt printed acknowledgement (on
a postcard!), but since then I have heard nothing.

I must ask you again, Sir, whether you intend to prosecute
'Penthouse' and Miss Crampton, and if not, why not.

Yours faithfully,

Henry Root

Henry Root.

Director of Public Prosecutions
4-12 Queen Anne's Gate London SW1H 9AZ

Telephone   Direct line 01-213   6142
Switchboard 01-213 3000

Mr. Harry Root
139 Elm Park Mansions
Park Walk
London
SW10

Your reference

Our reference
MDW/IP/MISC/3/79
Date
8 August 1979

Dear Sir

Thank you for your letter dated 7 August, 1979.

I do not intend to prosecute 'Penthouse' or
Miss Crampton, because in my view such a course
is not justified.

Yours faithfully

D. G. WILLIAMS

Assistant Director of Public Prosecutions

139 Elm Park Mansions
Park Walk
London, S.W.10.

Sir James Goldsmith,
Cavenham Foods,
Millington Road,
Hayes.   18th June 1979.

Dear Sir James,

    I've been watching you for some time and you're all right!
If you decide to go into politics you can count on at least one
vote. Mine!

    The way you stand up against the pinko conspirators in the
media is an inspiration to decent folk everywhere!

    If we stick together we can beat them. How much money do
they have? Not enough!

    Here's a pound. Although you always win your court cases
against the weasels of 'Private Eye' it's my experience that
cowardly bullies don't settle their bills as quickly as they prom-
ulgate an innuendo. The pound's to help you bridge the gap.

    I believe you're presently showing a high profile in the
publishing game. Well done! I'm about to go into publishing
myself with the purchase of the house of Cape. Do you know them?
All right once, not too sweet now. Perhaps we might get together
on this one. I'm looking for ▰▰ investors so if you're interested
why don't we grab a bite to eat some time?

    What do you say we meet for lunch at your favourite watering-
hole, the Clermont Club, on Friday 29th June? I'd make it sooner,
but I'm flat to the boards at the moment with one thing and another.

    I'm not a member of the Clermont myself, but no doubt you
can fix that. You get me in and I'll pay for lunch. How's that?
Fair enough?

    I look forward to meeting you on the 29th.

    Freedom of speech except for blackmailers! Let's go!

    Yours sincerely,

Henry Root

Henry Root.

139 Elm Park Mansions
Park Walk
London, S.W.10.

14th June 1979.

Mr A.R. Beevor,
Hambros Bank Ltd,
41 Bishopsgate,
London, E.C.2.

Dear Beevor,

Please forgive me for not having been back to you sooner
with reference to my take-over of Jonathan Cape Ltd.

The fact is I've been flat to the boards here trying to
raise the wind to get the caper off the ground.

Don't hesitate to let me know if you have any sharp ideas
yourself in this direction! I could use them!

Stay cool. I'll be back to you soon.

Yours sincerely,

Henry Root

Henry Root.

TELEPHONE: 01-480 5676.

65-68, LEADENHALL STREET
LONDON,
EC3A 2BA.

20th June 1979

Henry Root, Esq.,
139 Elm Park Mansions,
Park Walk,
London SW10

Dear Mr. Root,

Thank you very much for your letter which
I appreciated enormously. I am grateful for the
£1 which I will send to the appropriate charity
for retired journalists. I do so because I know
that the bulk of them are decent.

I wish you much good luck in your new venture.
At the moment I am fully involved in my own publishing
venture and I am afraid NOW magazine will take up all
the time and financial resources currently available!

Perhaps a little later in the year we can be in
touch again.

Yours sincerely,

James Goldsmith

139 Elm Park Mansions
Park Walk
London, S.W.10.

Mr Paul Johnson,
The Evening Standard,   30th May 1979.
Fleet Street,
London, E.C.4.

Dear Johnson,
        I would like you to know how much I appreciate your articles
in various newspapers and periodicals. More than any other journalist, you did more, it seems to me, to ensure that in the recent
election only a very small majority voted against Mrs Thatcher.

        I write to you now, in fact, concerning your article in
yesterday's 'Evening Standard', entitled 'Will Norman stop the
Tate dropping bricks?'

        'Of all Margaret Thatcher's appointments,' you wrote, 'the
one which I have heard most widely applauded - at any rate among
the London intelligensia - is her decision to give Norman St John
Stevas responsibility for the arts'.

        I don't doubt you're right, but can you tell me who precisely
constitutes 'the London intelligensia' and where they live? It
seems to me that they must be an exceptionally close-knit group, other-
all living in the same vicinity and meeting every evening, other-
wise even someone as well-connected as you could not, in the relatively short time since the election, have canvassed their opinion
of Norman's appointment.

        As a plain man who's kicked up it's never been my privilege
to meet 'London's intelligensia' and I'd like to put this right
before it's too late. Can you advise me how to set about it?

        A little later in the same article you say 'Norman is an
experienced boulevardier'. What's this exactly? I don't speak
much French, but a literal translation would seem to suggest that
Norman's an experienced street-walker. Can this really be the
case? Does Mrs Thatcher know?

        I'd be most grateful if you could clear up these two problems
for me. I wouldn't normally trouble such a busy and important
person with trivialities of this nature, but it's always struck
me that, though an aristocrat yourself, you care about the problems
of those you refer to as 'the people'.

        Yours sincerely,

        Henry Root

        Henry Root.

Copy to The Rt Hon Norman St John Stevas.

From PAUL JOHNSON, Copthall, Iver, Buckinghamshire, Iver 653350
                                          Saturday 7 July '79

Please accept my apologies for not having
answered your letter before. I have been in
Washington, then in the Middle East, and have
many unanswered letters. I have no secretary at
present — and large numbers of people write
to me, often posing questions I cannot answer.
A boulevardier is a man-about-town who knows his
way around; but how you are to meet the intelligensia is a query which cannot be satisfied
if it is necessary to prove it. P.J.

139 Elm Park Mansions
Park Walk
London, S.W.10.

The Officer-in-Charge,
The Criminal Record Office,
New Scotland Yard,
London, S.W.1.

30th May 1979.

Sir,

I would be grateful if you would run the following people
through the computor at Hendon and let me know whether they all
come up brand new. I don't think my reasons for wanting this
information need concern you. Suffice it to say that they are
people with whom I may be coming into contact, socially or in
a business context, in the near future.

Mr Ray Cooney. Impresario and immigrant (possibly illegal).
c/o The Whitehall Theatre, London.

Mr Edward du Cann. MP and one-time chairman of Keyser Ull-
mann Ltd of Milk Street, E.C.1. (not an address to inspire confidence). Rumoured to be descended from Miss Nell Gwynne.

Mr Russell Harty Plos. Chat show host. London Weekend
Television Ltd, London, S.E.1.

Mr Norman St John Stevas. Minister for 'the Arts'. Alleged
to be a boulevardier (or streetwalker.)

Mr Jonathan Cape (deceased). Publisher. Late of 30 Bedford
Square, London, W.C.1.

Mr Richard West. Cricket commentator, Rugby correspondent of
'The Times', one time 'host' of 'Come Dancing' and presently Morals
Correspondent of 'The Spectator', 56 Doughty Street, London, W.C.1.

Thanking you.

Yours faithfully,

Henry Root

Henry Root.

139 Elm Park Mansions
Park Walk
London, S.W.10.

The Officer in Charge,
Criminal Records Office,
New Scotland Yard,
London, S.W.1.

16th June 1979.

Dear Sir,

Did you get my letter of 30th May asking you to feed certain people through your computor at Hendon?

I imagine you can't have done, otherwise I would have heard from you by now.

If it always took as long as this to check out someone's deep background and personal standards you'd never catch anyone, least of all other policemen!

They'd be up and away while you were waiting for the print-out!

Let me know if you didn't get my letter and I'll send you a copy.

Yours faithfully,

Henry Root

Henry Root.

139 Elm Park Mansions
Park Walk
London, S.W.10.

The Officer-in-Charge,
Criminal Records Office,
New Scotland Yard,
London, S.W.1.

3rd July 1979.

Dear Sir,

I've been sitting here wondering why you haven't replied to my letters of 30th May and 16th June, requesting you to feed certain 'faces' through your computor.

Now I know! I should have bunged you!

Reporting the case of The Police and The Playboy Club v Ladbrooks Ltd in the matter of the Gaming Act, today's 'Daily Express' tells us that for a private citizen to obtain confidential information from the computor a 'drop' of 50p per name is levied by the policeman in charge.

Sorry! I should have been cognisant of this.

Although there were six names on my list originally, my own 'people' have been able to discover all anyone would want to know about Mr Richard West and Mr Russell Harty Plos. I now only need the deep background on Mr Ray Cooney, Mr Edward Du Cann, Mr Norman St John Stevas and Mr Jonathan Cape.

I enclose £2 being 50p for each name.

Sorry about my ignorance of the 'system'.

Yours faithfully,

Henry Root

Henry Root.

The Commanding Officer,
'B' Division (the best!),
Chelsea Police Station,
2 Lucan Place,
London, S.W.3.

139 Elm Park Mansions
Park Walk
London, S.W.10.

Dear Commander,

21st July 1979.

Over the past few weeks I have been corresponding with the
Criminal Records Office at Scotland Yard re getting the deep background on certain people with whom I was about to come in contact.

Receiving no reply to my letters, I eventually sent them a
couple of pounds to 'aid the due processes', as it were.

On the morning of Friday 13th July, two of your best men
(an Inspector and a Sergeant) ran trough my door with two pounds
in an envelope and pointed out that 'dropping' the CRO wasn't
good form.

Fair enough. However, they also pointed out that I had
wasted their valuable time. Being a great supporter of Law and
Order (particularly in Chelsea) I feel rather bad about this.
In the circumstances I would like to make a contribution to a
police charity which is on the up-and-up and I consequently now
return the two pounds. I recently sent a fiver to Sir David
McNee and he popped it into the Police Dependants' Trust. That
would be fine by me.

The post being what it is these days (don't worry - Sir
Keith Joseph will get that right), I'd like to hear that the
money has arrived safely, but please don't bother to send any
of your young men round to thank me personally.

Yours sincerely,

Henry Root

Henry Root.

139 Elm Park Mansions
Park Walk
London, S.W.10.

Sir Joseph Cantley,
Carpmael Buildings,
Temple,
London, E.C.4.   6th July 1979.

M'Lud,

    Now that the dust's settled after the so-called 'Trial of
the Century', I judge it to be the time to congratulate you on
the fine showing you put up throughout. You tipped the jury
the right way and some of your jokes were first-class! Well done!

    Some folk thought Thorpe was for the high jump at last, but
you never looked to me like the sort of man who'd send an Old
Etonian to the pokey on the say-so of an Italian air-line pilot,
a discredited businessman with dyed hair from L.A. (Los Angeles)
a dusky-hued character from the Channel Islands and a 'male model'
with the unlikely name of Josiffe.

    What a courageous example Mrs Thorpe set by the way she 'stood
by' her husband throughout his ordeal! (Perhaps you could have
made more of this in your closing speech for the defence). Most
wives would have popped the family valuables and had it away on
their toes to South America. And where, might I ask, were the
wives of Bessell, Josiffe and 'Gino' Newton? Conspicuous by their
absence!

    Here's a pound. I would have sent it to you during the trial,
but I was advised that you might rule this contempt of court and
pack me off with my tooth-brush for a night or two in Brixton! It
might also have been construed as an attempt to pervert the course
of justice, and I knew I could safely leave that to you.

    Yours respectfully,

    Henry Root

    Henry Root.

The Commissioner,
The City of London Police,
26 Old Jewry,
London, E.C.2.

139 Elm Park Mansions
Park Walk
London, S.W.10.

Dear Commissioner,

24th July 1979.

Some two weeks ago I had occasion to send a pound to Mr
Justice Cantley. This was a token of my esteem following the
way he conducted himself during the so-called Thorpe trial.

Imagine my surprise, last Friday morning, when two of
your officers returned this money in person on the grounds
that His Lordship didn't need it at the moment. They were
most courteous, of course, but did murmur something about it
being a waste of time and money having to hop round to my
place personally. Being a great supporter of the force (and
a friend of Mr James Anderton, the Chief Constable of Manchester) I was somewhat shocked to think that I of all people
had been responsible for using up the time of two fine young
officers who would have been better employed clearing our
streets of punks, muggers and demonstrating mimes on their
way to pester Mrs Thatcher re VAT.

In the circumstances, I am now returning the pound (it
may not be the same one, I'm afraid - money slips through the
fingers so quickly these days, don't you find?) and I would
be most pleased if you'd put it towards some worthy police
charity.

I'd like to ₍know₎ that this small contribution to the fight
against orchestrated extremism has arrived safely (the post
being what it is these days - no marks to Sir William Barlowe!),
but please don't bother to send any of your men round to thank
me personally. Frankly the sudden presence in my lounge-room
of two young constables on duty can have a negative bearing on
a business deal. I'm sure you'll understand.

Yours sincerely,

Henry Root
Henry Root.

Telephone 01-606 8866
Ext.

Telegrams ADJUTOR. LONDON. TELEX

Official Letters to be addressed:
THE COMMISSIONER OF POLICE
FOR THE CITY OF LONDON.

Please quote Ref.   F.14/80
Your Ref.

CITY OF LONDON POLICE,
26, OLD JEWRY,
LONDON, EC2R 8DJ.

6th August, 1979

Dear Mr Root,

I am directed by the Commissioner of
Police for the City of London to thank you
for your letter of 24th July, 1979 and
acknowledge safe receipt of your kind donation
of £1.00, which has been allocated to the
City of London Police Benevolent Fund as you
requested.

Yours sincerely,

A. Martin.

A/Chief Superintendent

H Root Esq
139 Elm Park Mansions
Park Walk
London SW10

139 Elm Park Mansions
Park Walk
London, S.W.10.

Mr Kenneth Kendall,
BBC News,
Lime Grove,   12th July 1979.
London, W.12.

Dear Kenneth,
        I hope you won't mind my calling you Kenneth. Your face
has been appearing for so long in my lounge-room that I feel
you're a friend of the family. Still, I expect that's what
they all say.
        Sorry to read in the paper today that your teeth fell out
while you were reading the news last night. Most awkward for
you.
        Here's a pound. Get yourself a tube of Dentu-Fix, but be
careful where you keep it. Mrs Snipe, who lives opposite, confused hers with the Polyfilla tube and all her windows fell out.
        How about a photo for Mrs Root? You're her favourite
newscaster. Do you merely read the news or do you make it up
as well? I've often wondered.
        All the best,
        Yours sincerely,

        Henry Root

        Henry Root.

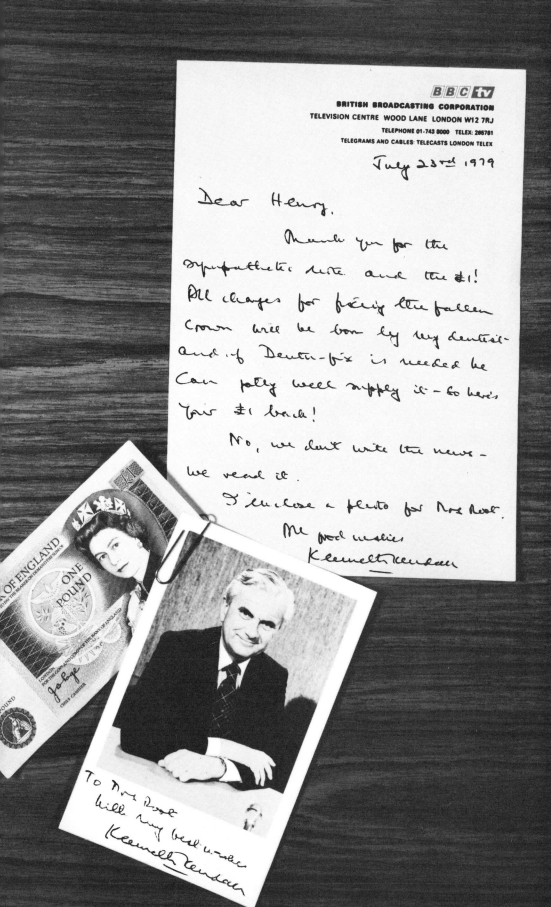

BBC tv

BRITISH BROADCASTING CORPORATION
TELEVISION CENTRE WOOD LANE LONDON W12 7RJ
TELEPHONE 01-743 8000 TELEX: 265781
TELEGRAMS AND CABLES: TELECASTS LONDON TELEX

July 23rd 1979

Dear Henry,

Thank you for the sympathetic note and the £1! All charges for fixing the fallen crown will be born by my dentist - and if Denture-fix is needed he can jolly well supply it - so here's your £1 back!

No, we don't write the news - we read it.

I enclose a photo for Mrs Root.

With good wishes

Kenneth Kendall

To Mrs Root
with my best wishes
Kenneth Kendall

139 Elm Park Mansions
Park Walk
London, S.W.10.

Lord Ted Dexter,   18th July 1979.
The Sunday Mirror,
Holborn Circus,
London, E.C.1.

My Lord!
        Your articles in 'The Sunday Mirror' are often good, as are
your live commentaries on TV. Well done! It seemed to me that
after lunch in the last Test you had difficulty getting your tongue
round the names of our Indian friends. Here's a tip. Don't bother
with their names. Just say: "Oh dear! The ball went straight
through the little sooty's legs!" That sort of thing.

        I write to you now to ask your opinion of our present skipper,
Brearley. He is more to blame than anyone, it seems to me, for the
introduction of compulsory crash helmets when batting. I appreciate
that he's an intellectual and as such will not wish to have his
brains rattled too often by a piece of hard leather travelling at
speed, but how many of those under him are intellectuals? None at
all, I'd guess, least of all the lad Botham and the big man, Hendrick.
'Rags' too strikes me as being alert in the field rather than a deep
thinker. So what's their excuse? I myself have been hit on the
head many times and this didn't stop me getting to the top in fish.

        I was concerned too by certain passages in Brearley's book
now being serialised in 'The Observer'. On the recent tour of
Australia horse-play took place, it seems, with the skipper's
approval, with the lad Botham putting himself about the English
dressing-room and introducing ice-cubes into Boycott's socks. Did
this sort of thing go on in your day? Surely not!

        I'm not happy either about all the pansy kissing and hand-
holding which now takes place in the middle, particularly at the
fall of a wicket. The photo above Brearley's article in yesterday's
'Observer' of Botham clasping the boy Gower to his bosom might well
have been misconstrued by those of a mind to do so.

        What's your opinion of these developments?

        Could you oblige with a photo? I'd like to stick it up in
my boy Henry Jr's room as an example of what can be done with an
upright stance and a straight bat. You were a true Corinthian and
some of your drives through mid-off would, on contact, have loosened
a rhino's balls. Of how many can one say that these days?

        Yours ever,

        Henry Root

        Henry Root.

5 Warwick Dene.
Ealing Common.
London. W5 3JG
01-567 3206.

Monday.

Dear Mr Root,

I don't keep prices about the place these days - sorry

How your lad goes the right way with his cricket.

Keep him <u>sideways</u> both batting and bowling.

I never see people make many runs with helmets!

Sincerely

Ted Dexter

139 Elm Park Mansions
Park Walk
London, S.W.10.

Mr Peter Saunders,
The Mousetrap Man!,
The Vaudeville Theatre,
London, W.C.2.

23rd July 1979.

Dear Mr Saunders,

May I be the first to congratulate you on your engagement to
the TV personality, Lady Katie Boyle? She's still a handsome woman
and her advice at the back of 'The TV Times' is sometimes sound.

That's enough of that - down to business! As far as I know
you've never put on a dirty show (well done!) so I am now enclosing
for your evaluation my original stage play THE ENGLISH WAY OF DOING
THINGS by HENRY ROOT. You'll find it an amusing romp in two acts
with only enough unnecessary explicitness to suck in our Japanese
friends over here to photograph Her Majesty and buy their underwear
in Oxford Street.

I'd be prepared to take your theatre for a season on sensible
terms. I read in 'The Sunday Express' the other day that you keep
in your office a fridge full of champagne for visiting actors and
other more serious folk, so unless I hear from you to the contrary
I'll drop in on you at about 11.30 on Tuesday 7th August to discuss
the deal. This will give you more than a week to assess the play's
potential and jot down casting ideas (though I'll have the final
say, of course, in this department.)

Have you come across the work of an actress called Glenda
Jackson? She'd be fine for the part of the old boiler who comes
to grief early in Act 1, but don't waste your time considering
'Sir' Robert Mark for the role of the stupid Police Commissioner
because he's already turned it down on the grounds that he doesn't
after all want to be an actor (after his TV deodorant commercial
who's surprised?)

I'd want first crack at the ingenue, of course, but you could
be second cab off the rank. I'd not say a word to your good lady
as long as you didn't drop me in it with Mrs Root!

Who gets the ice-cream sales? Do we share? I'll take care
of the critics. A fiver's on its way to Irving Warble of 'The Times'
and since Mrs Root is about to join Arriana Stassinopulos's 'Levi-
tation and Deep Personal Awareness' group I'll be able to 'get to'
Bernard Levin.

Let's make money here!

Yours for family theatre,

Henry Root

Henry Root.

Enc: THE ENGLISH WAY OF DOING THINGS by HENRY ROOT.

PETER SAUNDERS LTD

DIRECTORS: PETER SAUNDERS (CHAIRMAN & MANAGING) L. H. MITCHELL F.C.A. VERITY HUDSON
REGISTERED ENGLAND 507331

Tele 01-240 3177 (all lines)
Telegrams & Cables Saunplays London WC2

VAUDEVILLE THEATRE OFFICES
10, Maiden Lane, London, WC2E 7NA

30th July 1979

GEN/SH/86

Henry Root Esq
139 Elm Park Mansions
Park Walk
LONDON   SW10

Dear Mr Root

Thank you for your letter of the 25th July and for your congratulations.

Please don't come in on the 7th August as firstly, as I have a meeting which will last most of the day and secondly, I have quite a stock of plays to read and it is better to see if I like it first.

Yours sincerely

PETER SAUNDERS

PETER SAUNDERS LTD

DIRECTORS: PETER SAUNDERS (CHAIRMAN & MANAGING) L. H. MITCHELL F.C.A. VERITY HUDSON
REGISTERED ENGLAND 507331

Tele 01-240 3177 (all lines)
Telegrams & Cables Saunplays London WC2

VAUDEVILLE THEATRE OFFICES
10, Maiden Lane, London, WC2E 7NA

5th September 1979

GEN/SH/PLA

Henry Root Esq
139 Elm Park Mansions
Park Walk
LONDON   SW10

Dear Mr Root   "The English Way Of Doing Things" by Henry Root

Thank you for sending me this play but I don't think it is one that I would care to take on especially as I have another attraction to follow the current one at the Vaudeville.

Of course, I do indeed know Glenda Jackson but she has committed herself to another play in February of next year.

I am so sorry not to be more helpful but I don't think a meeting would really serve any purpose.

Yours sincerely

PETER SAUNDERS

Enc

139 Elm Park Mansions
Park Walk
London, S.W.10.

Ms Debra Byron,
Jonathan Cape Ltd,
30 Bedford Square,
London, W.C.1.

29th August 1979.

Dear Ms Byron,

You'll be wondering why you haven't heard from me since your sensible letter of 6th June.

Don't worry! I've been hard at work on a money-making concept that could do us both a bit of good.

Have you by any chance heard of a book entitled 'Man Watching' by a keeper at the London Zoo called Desmond Morris? I imagine you may have done because your outfit published it. It's a psychological pot-boiler, lacking that certain something to take it to the top of the hot-hundred list, but at least it had the merit of giving me this solid idea.

How about WOMAN WATCHING by HENRY ROOT? What do you think? And it would have the added advantage of being comprehensively illustrated by myself. You may not be aware that as well as being a writer I am also a fully equipped photographer of style ever at the ready with my system set, so I am taking this opportunity of enclosing my portfolio of girls snapped from an unexpected angle.

Here's the scheme. Financed by you I'll lurk unusually in places not normally available to men. No doubt you will yourself have visited 'The Sanctuary' in Covent Garden, a 'girls only' sauna and swimming club where dancers and others of that ilk strip off and recline on benches. With a letter of introduction from you, I'll hop incognito through the door in a pair of ballet pumps and, with a cry of "Straighten up ladies! I've been sent by Cape!", I'll take unusual photos before ejection.

How does it strike you? Let's be positive on this one!

What I need is a letter of authority from you enabling me to enter premises not generally available for figure shooting in the afternoon. I suggest something along the following lines:

TO WHOM IT MAY CONCERN:

This is to confirm that Mr Henry Root is engaged for us on a viable undertaking entitled WOMAN WATCHING. We would be most grateful if you could give him your full cooperation and, after he has finished, forward the account to us for settlement.

Signed: Debra Byron.
p.p. Jonathan Cape Ltd.

With your help I should be able to have the first draft on your desk by the end of October.

Let's go!

Yours sincerely,

Henry Root

Henry Root.

P.S. In case you're of a mind to utilise my photos to illustrate other books in your pipe-line, I should warn you that they are fully protected by the Copyright Act 1959, and I enclose a stamped addressed envelope for their safe return.

Telephone 01 636 5764
Telex 299080
Answer CBCSER G

JONATHAN CAPE LIMITED
THIRTY BEDFORD SQUARE
LONDON W.C.1

Telegrams
CAPAJON. LONDON WC1B 3EL

DB/ME

Mr Henry Root,
139 Elm Park Mansions,
Park Walk,
London. S.W.10.

31st August, 1979

Dear Mr Root,

Thank you for your letter of 29th August together with photographs.
We regret that we do not think it would be worth your while sending
us a finished copy of WOMAN WATCHING. We wish you sucess in placing
it elsewhere.

Please find your photographs enclosed.

Yours sincerely,

Debra Byron,
Editorial.

DIRECTORS: Tom Maschler Graham C. Greene Liz Calder W. Robert Carr Anthony Colwell John Robinson · Norman Askew
Registered in England under no. 195767. Registered office as above

139 Elm Park Mansions
Park Walk
London, S.W.10.

The Headmaster,
Langley Grammar School,
Langley,
Berks.   27th July 1979.

Dear Headmaster,

My friend Paul Johnson - who, as you may or may not know,
is one of Mrs Thatcher's closest advisers - recently wrote in
'The Evening Standard' that your school isn't a seminary for
subversives, has no great reputation for Marxist studies, drugs
or violence and that its staff do not spend their spare time
engaged in race-demos and assaults on the police.

Well done!

In the circumstances I'm prepared to entrust to your care
my boy Henry Jr, now 15. Frankly, he's not shaping up. He wears
girls' blouses and plays the guitar to excess. We all know where
that leads. A recent study shows that <u>one hundred per cent</u> of
youngsters on hard drugs had at some time in their lives listened
to so-called pop music.

When can he start? On the assumption that you believe in
private enterprise, I enclose a fiver. This is for you personally,
you understand, and is merely the tip of the ice-berg. There's
more to come if you manage to slip him to the top of the queue.

I'll pay generously for what I want, so if there's anything
you need - a new pav for the playing fields, perhaps, or a colour
TV for the Senior Common Room - just let me know.

Shall I come and see you? Just give me the word and I can
be your way in 24 hours.

I look forward to doing business with you.

How are you off for fish?

Support Mrs Thatcher!

Yours sincerely,

Henry Root

Henry Root.

P.S. I take it capital punishment still takes place in your school.
Let me know about this. Youngsters must learn what's what.

Langley Grammar School

Reddington Drive, Langley, Slough, SL3 7QS
Telephones:
Headmaster—Slough 43222 Staff—Slough 43223

Headmaster:

A. G. Robinson, M.Sc., Ph.D., C.Chem., F.R.I.C.

16 August 1978

Henry Root Esq
139 Elm Park Mansions
Park Walk
London SW 10

Dear Mr Root

Thank you for your letter of the 27 July enquiring about a possible
place here for Henry Junior.

The only possible suggestion which I cna make is that we test Henry
here at the school with a view to him entering our 5th year.   The
criterion for entry is usually the 12+ selection test conducted by
the Berkshire County Council.   The staff would be prepared to test
him at this stage in the various subjects.   If he was successful a
place would be offered.   You would then have to write to the Director
of Education at Kennet House, King's Road, Reading, with a view to
having this confirmed.   The difficulty would be the fact that you
reside in Greater London and this means taking the matter up with
them as well.

We assemble back for the Autumn Term on Tuesday, September 4th and if
you wished us to proceed with the testing this will be arranged.
Perhaps you would kindly let me know if you wish this to take place.

I am on holiday 17 - 31 August so if you contacted me on the phone
here at the school, Slough 43222, on Tuesday 4 September I will then
be in a position to suggest a date for testing.

Many thanks for your kind comments about the school.   I am forwarding
your £5 to the treasurer of the Langley Grammar School Fighting Fund
and he will send you a receipt in due course.

Looking forward to seeing you.

Yours sincerely

pp A. G. Robinson

Headmaster

Dictated by Dr Robinson but signed in his absence.

AN.

139 Elm Park Mansions
Park Walk
London, S.W.10.

The Senior Tutor,
Magdalene College,   29th July 1979.
Cambridge.

Dear Senior Tutor,

Yours is a college at which brains are neither here nor there,
I'm told. Indeed, my enquiries lead me to understand that duffers
are more than welcome so long as their fathers measure up financially.

This being the case, I'm prepared to send my boy to you in
three years time. He's 15 now and shows every sign of needing all
the advantages money can buy. You'll have seen many like that.

I'll leave the subject to you. <u>Not</u> sociology.

Places are tight, I dare say, (many being snapped up at birth
by Etonians and such) but I'm prepared to pay 'over the top' to
achieve equality of opportunity. That's the Tory way. We voted
for Mrs Thatcher so that those of us who had indulged in prudent
house-keeping down the years could give their youngsters a flying
start.

I enclose a small cash advance (this is for you personally,
you understand) against a heavy financial contribution to the
college if you can 'fix' a place for my boy.

What do you need? Do you have a decent library? If not,
just say the word. I'd be happy to endow you with sufficient
funds to build one. I'd want some sort of credit, of course.
Something along the lines of 'This Library has been generously
gifted to the College by Henry Root Wet Fish Ltd'. If you wanted
to put this in Latin, that would be okay with me. Or what about
a new pavillion for your playing-field? What, come to that, about
a new playing-field? Exercise, in my experience, takes boys' minds
off matters on which they'd be better not to dwell till later.

I look forward to hearing from you.

Yours against student participation,

Henry Root

Henry Root.

T. E. B. HOWARTH, M.C., M.A.,
SENIOR TUTOR AND TUTOR FOR ADMISSIONS

MAGDALENE COLLEGE
· CAMBRIDGE CB3 0AG
TELEPHONE 61543

31 July 1979

Henry Root Esq.,
139 Elm Park Mansions,
Park Walk,
London S.W.10.

Dear Mr. Root,

    Thank you for your letter. I am afraid I do not know who you are, but you are
evidently either an ingenious hoaxer or labouring under a massive misapprehension.
I therefore return your £5 note herewith.

    Yours sincerely,

139 Elm Park Mansions
Park Walk
London, S.W.10.

Major-General Wyldbore-Smith, C.B., D.S.O., O.B.E.,
Conservative Board of Finance,
32 Smith Square,   7th August 1979.
Westminster,
London, S.W.1.

Dear Major-General Wyldbore-Smith,

I'm a blunt man, accustomed to plain-speaking, so I'll come straight to the point.

What's the going price for getting an honour?

I'm not talking about an M.B.E., an O.B.E. or a C.B.E. They seem to be for ballet dancers, disc-jockeys, crooners and those who are quick over the high hurdles. (No offence meant. I see that you yourself have the O.B.E. Nothing wrong with that. Well done!) No, I'm talking about a life peerage, or, at the very least, a knighthood like my friend Sir James Goldsmith.

In the course of the past year I have contributed steadily and generously to Tory Party funds. Your understrapper Brigadier L.H. Lee C.B.E. will confirm this. (I am writing to you rather than him, incidentally, because you seem to outrank him and because you have the more sensible name.) I realise, however, that I will have to think in terms of a rather more substantial lump sum in order to secure a place near the top of Mrs Thatcher's New Year hand-outs.

Can you give me an idea of the approximate amount?

I read recently that a 'drop' of as little as £25,000 to one of our leading politicians was enough to obtain a seat in the Lords for the donor.

Has inflation bumped up the price?

Let me know. I'm waiting here with my cheque-book ready!

Support Mrs Thatcher!

Yours sincerely,

Henry Root

Henry Root.

P.S. It goes without saying that there could be 'something in this' for you personally.

CONSERVATIVE BOARD OF FINANCE

Chairman:
R ALISTAIR McALPINE

Director
MAJOR-GENERAL F.B. WYLDBORE-SMITH,
C.B., D.S.O., O.B.E.

Deputy Director
BRIGADIER L.H. LEE, C.B.E.

32 SMITH SQUARE,
WESTMINSTER, SW1P 3HH
TELEPHONE 01-222 9000

14th August 1979

Henry Root Esq.,
139 Elm Park Mansions
Park Walk
London SW10

Dear Mr. Root,

    Thank you for your letter of the 7th August. I think I must make it absolutely clear that there is no question of buying Honours from the Conservative Party.

    However, I am most grateful to you for the support which you have given to the Party over the past few months.

Yours sincerely,

F.B. Wyldbore-Smith

139 Elm Park Mansions
Park Walk
London, S.W.10.

Mr Simon Dally,
Weidenfeld & Nicolson Ltd,
91 Clapham High Street,
London, S.W.4.   16th June 1979.

Dear Mr Dally,

       Many thanks for your kind letter of 13th June.

       I appreciate your offer and encouraging remarks about my
book, but I'm afraid I have to tell you that I have thought it
best to put the whole matter into the hands of an experienced
literary agent.

       I am now exclusively represented by Miss Hilary Rubinstein
of A.P. Watt & Son (perhaps you know her) and I must ask you to
do nothing until you hear from her.

       Yours sincerely,

       Henry Root

       Henry Root.